TOLKIEN'S ART

By the same author

THE GENIUS FIGURE IN ANTIQUITY AND THE MIDDLE AGES

TOLKIEN'S ART
'A Mythology for England'

JANE CHANCE NITZSCHE

First edition 1979
First published in Papermac 1980

Published by
THE MACMILLAN PRESS LTD
London and Basingstoke
Associated companies in Delhi
Dublin Hong Kong Johannesburg Lagos
Melbourne New York Singapore Tokyo

Printed in Hong Kong

British Library Cataloguing in Publication Data

Nitzsche, Jane Chance
    Tolkien's art
    1. Tolkien, John Ronald Reuel – Criticism
and interpretation
    I. Title
    823'.9'12   PR6039.032Z/
    ISBN 0–312–80819–4
    ISBN 0–333–29034–8 (Papermac)

For Richard Franklin LeGrand
1957–1978

Contents

Acknowledgements

Chapter One, 'The Critic as Monster: Tolkien's Lectures, Prefaces, and Foreword', was delivered in a shortened form as a paper at the Twelfth Annual Medieval Conference, Western Michigan University, Kalamazoo, Michigan, on 7 May 1977. Portions of Chapter Two were delivered as a paper ('The Role of the Narrator in Tolkien's *Hobbit*: "The King under the Mountain"') at Rice University's English Department Reader-Response Colloquium, 3 February 1979; a slightly altered version of the same chapter appeared in *North Dakota Quarterly*, 47 (Winter 1979) 4–17. The Conclusion originated in a review published in the *Houston Chronicle*, Sunday *Zest Section* (11 September 1977) p. 13. Permission to reprint the above has been granted. Permission to quote from Tolkien's writings has been released by George Allen & Unwin (Publishers) Ltd and Houghton Mifflin Co. (for extracts from Tolkien's books); by the *Observer* (for extracts from a letter to the Editor, published on 20 February 1938); and by Mrs C. Meleck (for extracts from 'Beowulf: The Monsters and the Critics', first published in *Proceedings of the British Academy*, 1936).

I am indebted to Rice University's Fondren Library and its Inter-Library Loan Department for heroic efforts to obtain works by and about Tolkien. Rice University and the English Department generously provided a Summer Research Grant in 1976 which permitted me to complete the first three chapters; they also provided graduate and undergraduate assistance in the checking of transcriptions and documentation, and funds for the final typing

ACKNOWLEDGEMENTS

of the manuscript. Sue Davis produced a nearly error-free typescript from my rough copy. My colleagues Professor Will Dowden and Kathleen Murfin and good friend Candy MacMahon charitably volunteered to help me read page proofs, for which I am very grateful. The Macmillan Press, especially Mr Tim Farmiloe, Ms Julia Brittain, and Mrs Jean Kennedy, helped in many ways, not least of which was obtaining permissions on my behalf and producing this book so efficiently and well in such good time.

Thanks are extended to my good friend Jackie Boyd Schriver and to former graduate student Thad Logan for their care in reading portions of this work and making tough but necessary criticisms, and to Randel Helms, who commented in detail upon the first chapter and generally encouraged my progress with the book. I am especially grateful to those students and friends, Jay Rudin in particular, who supplied the stimulus for this study in the Lovett College course on Tolkien which I taught at Rice in the spring of 1976, and who wholly convinced me, had I any doubts left, that Tolkien is a major writer. My greatest debt is to Richard Franklin LeGrand, whose moral support and warm friendship and love helped me to complete this book. To his memory it is dedicated.

Houston, Texas   J.C.N.
March 1979

Introduction

You will be both grieved and amused to hear that out of about 60 reviews only 2 showed any knowledge that my idea of the fall of the Bent One was anything but an invention of my own. But if there only was someone with a richer talent and more leisure I think that this great ignorance might be a help to the evangelisation of England; any amount of theology can now be smuggled into people's minds under cover of romance without their knowing it.

C. S. Lewis
Letter to a Lady, 9 July 1939[1]

It is popularly believed that the hobbit stories narrated to his children 'conquered and remade Tolkien's imagination' to the point of 'reshaping even his responses to the literature he studied as Rawlinson Professor of Anglo-Saxon at Oxford' as well as influencing his theories of mythological imagination implemented in his later creative works.[2] This belief, however, perhaps confuses source with influence. In his distinguished biography Humphrey Carpenter reveals that Tolkien regarded himself not as 'an inventor of story' but as a 'discoverer of legend'.[3] That is, he attempted to 'discover', in his own words, a

> body of more or less connected legend, ranging from the large and cosmogonic to the level of romantic fairy-story – the larger founded on the lesser in contact with the earth, the lesser drawing splendour from the vast backcloths – which I could dedicate simply: to England, to my country.[4]

The earliest expression of his discovery was a poem written in 1914

1

after a vacation in Cornwall, 'The Voyage of Earendel the Evening Star', later to become Chapter Twenty-Four of 'Quenta Silmarillion', the long middle section of *The Silmarillion*. Such expressions were intended to provide a historical and poetic context for the private languages of Quenya or High-elven and Sindarin or Common Elvish he had begun constructing in 1912, languages which he modelled upon Finnish and Welsh respectively, and which were themselves inspired by his exploration of the Northern mythologies of the Elder and Prose Eddas.[5] But the poem itself was inspired by a line from Cynewulf's Old English *Crist*, 'Eala Earendel engla beorhtost' ('Behold Earendel brightest of angels').[6] Neither the religious subject-matter of Cynewulf's poem which attracted Tolkien nor the Old English language in which it was written should come as a surprise: Tolkien was devoutly Roman Catholic in belief and of course eventually a professor at Oxford who loved, taught, and published research on Old and Middle English literature. It seems appropriate that the seeds for his 'mythology for England' sprang from those medieval literary, religious, and cultural ideas in which his life was steeped.

His publications on medieval English literature begin as early as 1925 with an edition of *Sir Gawain and the Green Knight*, followed by an essay on the *Ancrene Wisse* and *Hali Meiðhad* in 1929. These publications precede *The Hobbit* (1937), in fact begun in 1931, although his children had heard some episodes from it before 1930.[7] Indeed, when asked about the sources of *The Hobbit* he replied, in a letter published in the *Observer* on 20 February 1938, that it derived from 'epic, mythology, and fairy-story'. Specifically he acknowledges that '*Beowulf* is among my most valued sources; though it was not consciously present to the mind in the process of writing, in which the episode of the theft arose naturally (almost inevitably) from the circumstances . . .' He adds that his tale *was* consciously based on the then unpublished *Silmarillion*, a 'history of the Elves'. If he wished to develop a 'mythology for England' akin to the Northern mythologies of the Eddas, what better way to use those Old and Middle English works native to the country in fashioning his own works?

It is the general purpose of this study to show how his creative works reflect his interest in medieval English literature, especially Old English, as expressed through his scholarship on and critical studies of such works. Because his relatively minor fictive works reveal this dependence more clearly in some ways than his greatest, *The Lord of the Rings*, a larger proportion of the analysis than their literary value warrants will be devoted to discussions of *The Hobbit*, the fairy-stories 'Leaf by Niggle' and 'Smith of Wootton Major', and medieval parodies like *Farmer Giles of Ham*. They thus provide foils for the trilogy, in which medieval ideas metamorphose into art more successfully – and subtly. *The Silmarillion*, however, poses a critical problem in that it was begun in 1914 but although it might be viewed as an early and even minor work it was not finished during Tolkien's lifetime, existed in multiple recensions, and was only edited and published posthumously by Tolkien's son Christopher in 1977, four years after the author's death. It will therefore be treated as a late and even unfinished work possibly more influenced by, than influencing, other literary works published throughout his life, and certainly no longer expressing only the interests and ideas of his youth. As Christopher declares in his Foreword, these

> old legends ('old' now not only in their derivation from the remote First Age, but also in terms of my father's life) became the vehicle and depository of his profoundest reflections. In his later writing mythology and poetry sank down before his theological and philosophical preoccupations: from which arose incompatibilities of tone.[8]

Clearly source and influence become inextricably mixed in this work by Tolkien.

The most important scholarly study with parallels in the creative works is his 1936 Sir Israel Gollancz Lecture entitled 'Beowulf: The Monsters and the Critics' (published in the same year in an academic periodical and reprinted much later in a well-known *Beowulf*-studies anthology).[9] Although required reading for any *Beowulf* student, it has not yet appeared on the required reading list for *The Lord of the Rings*, a work many critics believe equal in stature to the Old English epic.

In the *Beowulf* lecture Tolkien attempted to resolve the long-standing critical debate over whether the poem was 'pagan' or Christian by concluding that it was *both*: Germanic heroic values and Christianity coexist within the epic. Tolkien's own works grapple with the same conflict: is a good warrior also a good man? Does a warrior owe primary allegiance to his lord (*dryhten*) or to the Lord (*Dryhten*)? It is the social role and religious image of the lord and king through which Tolkien expresses his deepest philosophical and theological ideas.

Significantly, Tolkien referred to the hero Beowulf and not to the poem *Beowulf* in the title of his seminal article, 'Beowulf: The Monsters and the Critics'. Why should the King Beowulf occupy such a central position in the title when the poem's monsters chiefly demand Tolkien's attention in the article? A pattern emerges upon an examination of the titles of other Tolkienian works. Either the title centres on the hero ('Beowulf',*The Hobbit*, 'Leaf by Niggle', 'Smith of Wootton Major', *The Adventures of Tom Bombadil*, *Farmer Giles of Ham*) or, antithetically, on the hero's chief adversary ('The Homecoming of Beorhtnoth Beorhthelm's Son', *The Lord of the Rings*, *The Silmarillion* – the history of the Silmarils, symbols of man's lowest desires). The specific purpose of this study is to explore the reasons for this pattern of heroic conflict by tracing the development of the adversary (the dragon, the monster, the critic, the king) through Tolkien's early works, culminating in the trilogy and *The Silmarillion*.

Irresponsible lordship – like that demonstrated by Beorhtnoth in the Old English poem, 'The Battle of Maldon', and criticised in Tolkien's verse drama, 'The Homecoming' – most troubles Tolkien. The lord often commands his men to die for him, not out of a zeal to protect the tribe, but out of pride, to boost his own name. The subordinate, acting out of love and loyalty, obeys his lord but tragically so when such obedience results in unnecessary death. Responsible lordship as exemplified in the sacrifice of one's own desires on behalf of others, especially the tribe, represents a healing and even redemptive act – symbolised by Aragorn's role in the House of Healing as he conveys the miraculous herb *kingsfoil* from wounded warrior to warrior, and of course by God the Father's role in offering his only son for sacrifice in order to heal mankind, Christ himself becoming, as medieval poets often called him, the archetypal Physician. The good lord, then, Tolkien usually casts in the role of healer or artist (healing and artistry both constructive acts, one physical, one spiritual) – but the evil lord he casts in the image of monster or dragon.

The Dragon in *Beowulf*, like Grendel, signifies the *feond mancynnes* (the enemy of mankind) and of God, so that the battle between Beowulf and the monsters on a higher level means that 'the real battle is between the soul and its adversaries' (p. 73). The figure of the monster externalises the evil within each soul. Hence it is the hero Beowulf and not the poem upon whom Tolkien focuses in the article's title. More anagogically, such a battle with a *feond* also signifies the conflict between man and his ultimate enemy, Death. Tolkien imagines the *Beowulf* poet surveying past heroes so that he 'sees that all glory (or as we might say "culture" or "civilization") end in night' (p. 73). In this world, as Germanic heroic values have it, 'man, each man and all men, and all their works shall die' (p. 73). So the *Beowulf* poet represents for Tolkien the hero of the title, an idea conveyed by the article's last line and final metaphor. Tolkien expresses his confidence in the permanence of *Beowulf*, given its similar language, geographical setting, and nationality of author – 'it must ever call with a profound appeal' – only, however, 'until the dragon comes' (p. 88). Even art will eventually perish before the final adversary of all creation, the antithesis of its Author – total annihilation. The Dragon thus concretely realises those allegorical personifications whom Milton portrayed as the offspring of Satan's mind in *Paradise Lost* – Sin and Death. It recurs, in varying form, throughout Tolkien's works.

In Tolkien's prose non-fiction, especially the lectures and fore-words, the 'monster' is the critic-scholar who prefers history and philology to art-for-art's-sake, reflecting by his choice a ratiocina-tion sterile, stale, and dead, in contrast to the alive and joyful imagination of the artist-hero with whom Tolkien identifies. This analogy is explored in Chapter One of this study, 'The Critic as Monster: Tolkien's Lectures, Prefaces, and Foreword'.

In Chapter Two, 'The King under the Mountain: Tolkien's Children's Story', the monster is the dragon Smaug in his role of King under the Mountain guarding dwarf treasure in *The Hobbit*. But more sentient monsters populate this children's story – Thorin the dwarf-king, the Master of Dale, and the Elvenking. Their heroic antagonist is the artist Bilbo who as the story progresses becomes increasingly skilful in his role as burglar. In addition the pompous narrator (criticised as an aesthetic flaw in studies of the novel) also emerges as a monster whose critical and patronising comments subvert the impact of the very story he narrates. Thus this children's story fictionalises the ideas in Tolkien's *Beowulf* and fairy-story lectures.

In Chapter Three, 'The Christian King: Tolkien's Fairy-Stories', the adversary is depicted as a more abstract monster: the critical neighbour Parish in 'Leaf by Niggle' and the unskilled but preten-tious Master Cook in 'Smith of Wootton Major'. Interestingly enough the artist as hero (Niggle and Smith) emulates the pattern of the archetypal artist, Christ as the Word, who is represented in the stories as the Second Voice in 'Leaf' and Alf the Faery-King in 'Smith'. Sacrificing one's art in order to help one's neighbour or renew society resembles the greatest sacrifice – of Himself – offered by the Son of God. In these stories Tolkien fictionalises ideas from his fairy-story lecture and the *Ancrene Wisse*.

In Chapter Four, 'The Germanic King: Tolkien's Medieval Parodies', Tolkien's excursions into mimesis in the parody of the Breton lay ('The Lay of Aotrou and Itroun'), Middle English romance and *fabliau* (*Farmer Giles of Ham*), Old English alliterative verse ('The Homecoming of Beorhtnoth Beorhthelm's Son'), and the *imram* or 'voyage' ('Imram') define the king in chivalric terms as a lord motivated by excessive pride to the detriment of his tribe and himself. His subordinate, whether a *ceorl* or a knight, represents a mock hero who symbolises the lower class rebelling against the aristocratic nonsense of the chivalric code. The 'monster' assumes a social as well as moral dimension. The parodies are modelled upon Breton lays, *Sir Gawain and the Green Knight,* the *Canterbury Tales*, 'The Battle of Maldon', and 'The Voyage of St Brendan'.

In Chapter Five, 'The Lord of the Rings: Tolkien's Epic', Sauron as archetypal and abstract Evil projects a monstrous adversary far more terrifying in his formlessness than the lesser adversaries described as leaders and kings – Saruman, Denethor, Boromir. (Sauron's fragmented self symbolises the divisiveness of his evil – his Eye searches the countryside while his Lieutenant as his Mouth addresses the free peoples at the Gate to Mordor.) Monsters whose evil suggests a more physical viciousness like wrath, gluttony, or avarice reflect this in their form – Balrog, Shelob, Gollum. In contrast, the human and elven kings who battle these monsters function more as servants than as masters – especially Aragorn, long disguised as the humble ranger Strider. The medieval conflict between the Germanic value of valour in battle to support one's lord, an expression of the virtue of obedience and love, and the Christian virtue of charity in sacrificial acts to support one's neighbour and Lord, Tolkien reconciles finally through the sacrificial (Christian) act of the free peoples, who heroically battle (in Germanic fashion) Sauron's Lieutenant to divert attention from the real threat to Sauron, the humble servant Sam who aids Frodo in his trek toward Mount Doom. This sacrificial act in macrocosm counterpoints Gollum's sacrifice of himself in battle with Frodo to save his master or lord – the Ring, to whom he has sworn fealty. However, the battle with Frodo is motivated not by the loving desire of the subordinate to support his lord but instead by his selfish desire to become his lord – an act of disobedience. In contrast the battle with the Lieutenant is motivated by the love of the masters and kings, specifically Gandalf and Aragorn, a love directed toward those seemingly unimportant halflings Sam and Frodo, who are themselves servants of the free peoples. The trilogy thus unifies many of the themes and concepts found in the minor works of Tolkien, which were themselves influenced by various medieval English poems and his own scholarship on them.

Finally, in the Conclusion Tolkien's posthumous *Silmarillion* will be examined as a 'Book of Lost Tales', a mythological collection whose emphasis on philology and history and whose debt to the Northern mythologies mark it as a work belonging to an early stage in the development of Tolkien's art, and whose biblical (Old Testament) morality thematically anticipates the more specifically Christian ethos found explicitly or implicitly in his other works. Nevertheless, it does exhibit the same religious themes of pride and fall and the same images and symbols of bad kingship analysed in those previous works, especially in the figures of Melkor, Sauron, Fëanor, and Ar-Pharazôn, but without the buttressing of Germanic heroic and chivalric concepts. As its mythology inspired the writing of later works, and as its publication ensures a complete history for the Middle-earth described in so many of his greatest works, it constitutes an appropriate coda to Tolkien's life as a philologist and historian, philosopher and theologian – and artist and mythologist.

1 The Critic as Monster: Tolkien's Lectures, Prefaces, and Foreword

When Tolkien delivered the Sir Israel Gollancz Memorial Lecture of 1936, he changed the course of *Beowulf* studies for the next forty years and also permanently altered our understanding of the Old English poem. As a scholarly article, 'Beowulf: The Monsters and the Critics' sought to demonstrate the coexistence of Germanic and Christian elements in the poem, especially in the figures of its monsters, Grendel and the Dragon, formerly viewed as peripheral to the work's main theme and structure. By so doing it provoked a controversy over its Germanic and Christian aspects that continues to rage today, although in more subdued fashion. As a work of prose non-fiction by a great writer, however, the article has been ignored.[1] This study seeks to illuminate the way in which the *Beowulf* article so fully catalysed Tolkien's imagination that few of his creative works escaped its explicit or implicit influence.

His article chiefly centres on three points: first, *Beowulfiana* is 'poor in criticism, criticism that is directed to the understanding of a poem as a poem'.[2] Previously scholars of Old English had investigated only its historical, folkloric, or philological importance and had not perceived the literary merits of the poem. Second, the responsibility for this lapse in aesthetic judgement rests solely with the critic lacking that mythic imagination the poem evokes and not with the poem itself. Third, when the critic does then examine the poem as a poem he wholly misunderstands it. To illustrate,

Tolkien cites W. P. Ker (cited in a passage by R. W. Chambers) who believes that *Beowulf*'s weakness lies in placing 'irrelevances' at the centre and 'serious things' on the outer edges (p. 59). By 'irrelevances', Tolkien explains, Ker means the monsters.

Such an adversary relationship between the *Beowulf* poet, the *Beowulf* critic, and the *Beowulf* monsters so captures Tolkien's imagination that he entitles this article 'Beowulf: The Monsters and the Critics'. If Beowulf as the hero battles with monsters (Grendel and the Dragon) and the critics who have misunderstood him (W. P. Ker and R. W. Chambers), then, Tolkien fantasises, the critics *are* the monsters – and Tolkien by defending Beowulf *is* the hero. This implicit fantasy is carefully developed through a series of metaphors in this article and becomes explicit in his Andrew Lang Lecture of 1938 on the subject of fantasy and fairy-stories.

The problem with this fantasy is that Tolkien himself as a critic remained interested in history and philology as is evident from his prefaces to critical editions and translations of medieval works. How can he identify with the hero opposing monstrous evil when he also occupies the role of the monster-critic? Tolkien provides an answer in the Foreword to *The Lord of the Rings*, in which he establishes himself both as a Frodo-like hero in his artistic role and, in his critical role pontificating upon the meaning of his own work, as a Saruman or Sauron-like monster. This divided self surfaces throughout Tolkien's fictive works and exists as a symbolic badge of man's fallen and imperfect nature. Man is good – but also evil, as *Beowulf* is Germanic – but also Christian. We turn first to an examination of the stages in Tolkien's development of his fantasy – and Fantasy – in the lectures.

I The Lectures: W. P. Ker and Andrew Lang as Monsters

Tolkien in the *Beowulf* article defends the 'irrelevances' of the poem – the monsters – responsible for that structural 'disproportion' so disliked by Ker. Seeing instead a 'balance' expressed as 'an opposition of ends and beginnings . . . a contrasted description of two moments in a great life, rising and setting; an elaboration of the ancient and intensely moving contrast between youth and age, first achievement and final death' (p. 81), he argues that the monsters reflect threats to Beowulf at two crucial moments in his life. As a young man the hero appropriately aids the Danish king

Hrothgar by successfully battling with the monster Grendel in the first half, or the 'rising moment', of the poem; and in the second half as an old king aids his Geats, so he thinks, by battling with the Dragon in the 'setting moment' of the poem and of his life.

As an adversary the Old English monster possesses three significations for Tolkien. In a Germanic sense it functions thematically as *feond mancynnes*, the enemy of mankind with whom such monsters ally in Nordic mythology – chaos, unreason, death and annihilation. Because it battles only with 'man on earth' it conveys the ancient theme 'that man, each man and all men, and all their works shall die . . . [the *Beowulf* poet] sees that all glory (or as we might say "culture" or "civilization") ends in night' (p. 73). In a Christian sense it represents the enemy of God as well as of man – sin and spiritual death. Although the poem should not be read as an allegory of the *miles Christi* who battles the Adversary with his breastplate of righteousness and shield of faith inherited from Ephesians 6, still the battle assumes Christian proportions: '. . . there appears a possibility of eternal victory (or eternal defeat), and the real battle is between the soul and its adversaries' (p. 73). In a modern sense, finally, the monster signifies the adversary of the *Beowulf* poem: the critic who misunderstands it because of his predilection for history and philology instead of art, for dead ratiocination instead of live imagination. Allegorically he represents the final adversary of mankind, the dragon Death fought by the artist with the weapon of his art in the hope that its eternal life will defeat this dragon – 'Death, *thou* shalt die.'

Although Tolkien develops the first two significations through plain expository prose, this last signification he develops through a cumulative sequence of five allegorical and metaphorical *exempla* interspersed throughout the article. The first *exemplum* portrays the poem *Beowulf* as a medieval hero on a journey-quest whose initiation is hampered by those allegorical guides supposedly helping him: those guides of history, philology, mythology, archaeology and laography represent the interests of modern scholars that stifle communication between the poem and its readers:

As it set out upon its adventures among the modern scholars, *Beowulf* was christened by Wanley Poesis – *Poeseos Anglo-Saxonicae egregium exemplum*. But the fairy godmother later invited to superintend its fortunes was Historia. And she brought with her Philologia, Mythologia, Archaeologia, and Laographia. Excellent ladies. But where was the child's name-sake? Poesis was usually forgotten; occasionally admitted by a side-door; sometimes dismissed upon the door-step. 'The Beowulf', they said, 'is hardly an affair of yours, and not in any case a protégé that you could be proud of. It is an historical document.' (pp. 52–3)

Poesis, or poetry-for-poetry's sake, as a humble and male servant (rather than an arrogant female master or superior) is denied access to the hero because he seems a pedagogical churl: the ladies sneer that '"Only as [a historical document] does [Beowulf] interest the superior culture of to-day"' (p. 53, my italics). In his low status he resembles other humble Tolkienian heroes or guides of heroes – Farmer Giles, Niggle, Smith, and the hobbits from their agrarian background. In contrast the ladies as effete scholars ally with such arrogant adversaries as King Augustus Bonifacius, Tompkins, Nokes, the Lord of the Rings, Sauron himself, and his former master Morgoth, or Melkor.

In his next exemplum Tolkien switches focus from poem to poet and transforms the supposedly helpful godmother and guides into 'friends' and 'descendants' of the poet (called merely 'a Man') who misunderstand and abuse him. The conflict centres now on a tower of old stones taken from a house of his father which the Man has built to 'look out upon the sea' – that is, figuratively to see better or to gain perspective or wisdom. But the friends and descendants view the tower differently: not interested in far-sightedness and perceptivity they refuse even to climb the steps and instead gaze myopically at their old stones. Wishing 'to look for hidden carv-ings' or to seek 'a deposit of coal under the soil' (p. 55), they seem as materialistic and short-sighted as the dwarves of The Hobbit and The Lord of the Rings. Their myopia mirrors their lack of spirituality: they fulfil their destructive, selfish inclinations by pushing over the tower, digging under its soil, and generally disregarding the moral and legal rights of the tower-builder. The parable intimates that modern critics (so-called 'Friends') and even modern poets ('Descendants') prefer discovery of its sources and influences (the stone blocks' hidden carvings and coal deposits) to enjoyment and use of the whole poem (tower) in order to attain insight about life (to climb its steps and view the sea). Their 'sensible' source-hunting overwhelms the tower-builder's delight in the 'nonsensi-

cal tower', as the friends term it. Unfortunately, he remains wholly
alone, his friends more unkind than any enemies, his descendants
more distant and alien than any strangers.

In the third *exemplum* the critic metamorphoses into the monster
of the jabberwock, an unnatural creature that symbolises the
perversion of those in the first two *exempla*. This creature creates
cacophony through a 'conflicting babel' of opinion: 'For it is of their
nature that the jabberwocks of historical and antiquarian research
burble in the tulgy wood of conjecture, flitting from one tum-tum
tree to another' (p. 56). They no longer constitute a physical danger
to others because of their myopia, which resembles that of the
'friends' and 'descendants': 'Noble animals, whose burbling is on
occasion good to hear; but though their eyes of flame may
sometimes prove searchlights, their range is short' (p. 56). Such
shortsightedness hints at a greater spiritual danger to themselves
as well as to others, for the 'conflicting babel' of their opinions
reminds us of the confusion of tongues at the Tower of Babel as the
epitome of the sin of pride (of course in the last *exemplum* the critics
destroyed the tower of the artist in *their* pride). Pride and selfishness, myopia, a 'conflicting babel' of opinion, destructiveness,
chaos, all characterise the critic—truly a monster.

By the fourth metaphor Tolkien can finally identify the conflict
he has portrayed abstractly thus far as a 'battle' between hero and
monster: '[Chambers] gives battle on dubious ground' (p. 65).
Chambers misunderstands the poem or 'battles' with it, because he
argues that the story of Ingeld, for example, remains a real centre
of *Beowulf*, its monsters mere 'irrelevances' (p. 59). However,
because Tolkien has depicted *Beowulf* and its poet as protagonists
(knight, tower-builder) and the critic as antagonist (false female
guide, false friend and tower-destroyer, jabberwock), it becomes
clear that Chambers 'gives battle on dubious ground' as a *monster*
rather than as a hero, whose role is occupied here by the true and
humble friend of the poem, Poesis itself or Tolkien, defender of
myth. Ironically, Chambers as critic-monster specifically opposes
the monsters of *Beowulf* – his adversary is as well Grendel and the
Dragon.

Further, the actual battle may not resemble a heroic contest
between two opponents so much as murder of an innocent animal
in the scientific laboratory of the experimenting vivisectionist. The
critic opposes the *Beowulf* monsters because as the rational man
he misunderstands and dislikes frivolity. Yet for Tolkien 'A dragon

is no idle fancy' but 'a potent creation of men's imagination' (p. 64).
Beowulf's Dragon can be criticised only because it does not seem
'dragon enough, plain pure fairy-story dragon' (p. 65). As a
personification of malice, greed, and destruction, or the evil side of
heroic life, it symbolises *draconitas*, an abstract idea and generic
type rather than a concretely depicted, individualised monster (p.
65). A 'plain pure fairy-story dragon' should not be explained or it
will die; so its defender, like the critic, '. . . unless he is careful,
and speaks in parables, . . . will kill what he is studying by
vivisection, and he will be left with a formal or mechanical
allegory, and, what is more, probably with one that will not work.
For myth is alive at once and in all its parts, and dies before it can
be dissected' (pp. 63–4). The rational man or the critic seems not
only a monster but a murderer, a homicide like Grendel.

As such the critic exercising his rational faculty must still battle
with the artist who delights in his imaginative faculty. For 'The
significance of a myth is not easily to be pinned on paper by
analytical reasoning. It is at its best when it is presented by a poet
who feels rather than makes explicit what his theme portends; who
presents it incarnate in the world of history and geography, as our
poet has done' (p. 63). Although he may die, his work, like the
dragon a 'potent creation of . . . imagination', will live on, mutely
battling with misunderstanding critics and the ravages of time and
death. In the last lines of the article Tolkien claims of *Beowulf* that it
will 'ever call with profound appeal' to those who live in England
and speak English because of its similar origin and language –
'until the dragon comes' (p. 88). That final critic in Tolkien's fifth
and final metaphor is the last dragon – complete chaos, complete
annihilation and darkness.

In the contemporaneous Andrew Lang Lecture of 1938, 'On
Fairy-Stories', he develops more explicitly the earlier implicit
fantasy concerning the adversary relationship between the artist
and the critic in the *Beowulf* article through a contrast between
himself as lover of fairy-stories and the analyst and compiler of
fairy-stories in the archetypal critic, Andrew Lang. In the short
preface to his Andrew Lang Lecture Tolkien sketches the 'over-
bold' lover of fairy-stories as a medieval romance hero seeking 'a
rash adventure', a 'wandering explorer' who grows inarticulate in
trying to report the 'richness and strangeness' of the land.[3] Such
an adventurer need not have 'studied them professionally', for
only a childlike wonder will result from these adventures in

Faërie. To approach Faërie as a professional seeking not wonder but information, like any lost adult on a trip, is to 'ask too many questions' so that the gates to Faërie will be shut and the keys lost (p. 3). Such a professional was Andrew Lang, who collected fairy-stories in twelve books of twelve different colours appearing in print as early as 1889. Because Lang's 'collections are largely a by-product of his *adult study* of mythology and folk-lore' (p. 36, my italics), he includes selections in his books inappropriate to the true fairy-story such as travellers' tales, dream tales, and beast fables, all in some way connected with the primary (real or adult) world. He regards a fairy-story as a means to an end rather than an end in itself – interesting as an example of the monkey's heart topos, but not interesting as a story. His interests are scientific (at least in intent): 'they are the pursuit of folklorists or anthropologists: that is of people using the stories not as they were meant to be used, but as a quarry from which to dig evidence, or information, about matters in which they are interested' (p. 18). In addition Lang so misunderstands the nature and purpose of fairy-stories that he intends his collections only for literal children, to be used to satisfy both the 'belief' in and 'appetite' for marvels of the young man (p. 36). But 'belief' and 'appetite' must be distinguished. As a child Tolkien experienced a desire for dragons (p. 41) but not for belief: '. . . at no time can I remember that the enjoyment of a story was dependent on belief that such things could happen, or had happened, in "real life" ' (p. 40). Further, Tolkien truly came to love fairy-stories *only as an adult*. 'It is parents and guardians', he admits, who like Lang (the latter addresses his collections to these parents because they and not their children possess the money to purchase them) 'have classified fairy-stories as *Juvenilia*' (p. 44). Both the parent and the scientist assume only the child can experience a desire for marvels.

Although Tolkien warns that 'The process of growing older is not necessarily allied to growing wickeder, . . . the two do often happen together' (p. 44). To combat this tendency adults must not play at being children who have never grown up but instead regain an innocence or wonder similar to that of the child in Wordsworth's 'Intimations of Immortality'. This wonder allows the adult to escape from the weariness of living in the primary world of the twentieth century with its burgeoning scientific and materialistic values and to experience the sudden joyous 'turn' of the eucatastrophic happy ending available in the sub-creation of the secondary world – in Literature as the antithesis of Drama. The latter is preferred by the critic because it reveals the dyscatastrophe inherent in tragedy and because, from the critic's point of view, it sheds the pretence that a secondary world exists beyond the primary one (p. 51). In the secondary world of fantasy Tolkien can realise his own 'happy ending' – the overthrow of the arrogant British critic – which he cannot in the real world.

This monstrous critic in the *Beowulf* lecture and the adult and scientific fairy-story collector in the fantasy lecture find satiric expression in the mock translator of a supposed obscure Latin work, Tolkien's medieval parody *Farmer Giles of Ham* (1949). As a critic the translator defends his decision to translate the 'curious tale' into English for a historical reason: it provides a glimpse into 'life in a dark period of the history of Britain, not to mention the light that it throws on the origin of some difficult place-names'.[4] As an afterthought he adds a lesser, literary, reason, probably one that would appeal to a child interested in marvels, but certainly not to an educated adult: 'Some may find the character and adventures of its hero attractive in themselves'. His interest is literary only in the sense that discussions of sources and influences are literary; he disparages the sources of the tale 'derived not from sober annals, but from the popular lays' (p. 7). Superior in his respect for and fidelity to the fact and truth of geography and history, he denigrates the author's skimpy geographical knowledge ('it is not his strong point') and his acquaintance with recent contemporary history ('For him the events that he records lay already in a distant past'). Ironically, he exposes his own supercilious ignorance of truth when he grudgingly admits that this author's voice must be authentic and the account true, for 'he seems . . . to have lived himself in the lands of the Little Kingdom'. Medieval literature, highly stylised and conventional, rarely reflected the autobiographical experience of any writer, many of whom are anonymous.

This critic's instructive and apologetic preface smacks of presumption. He seeks to guide the reader's response to the work and to interfere with the artist's relationship with his reader. Given Tolkien's distaste for the role of critic, what role does he assume in the prefaces and forewords to his own editions and translations of medieval works – and to his own artistic works, especially *The Lord of the Rings*?

II The Prefaces and the Foreword: Tolkien as Monster

As an artist Tolkien portrays himself as a hero and the artistic process as a journey-quest very like that of the *Beowulf* poem in the first *exemplum* of the *Beowulf* article or like Frodo's in *The Fellowship of the Ring*. In the 'Introductory Note' to *Tree and Leaf* (written when 'On Fairy-Stories' and 'Leaf by Niggle' were published together in 1964–5) he identifies himself as a childlike but heroic hobbit who wrote these two works 'when *The Lord of the Rings* was beginning to unroll itself and to unfold prospects of labour and exploration in yet unknown country as daunting to me as to the hobbits. At about that time we had reached Bree, and I had then no more notion than they had of what had become of Gandalf or who Strider was; and I had begun to despair of surviving to find out' (p. 2). This analogy between the role of the artist in the primary world and the role of the hero in the secondary world continues in the Foreword to *The Lord of the Rings*: 'In spite of the darkness of the next five years [1939–45], I found that the story could not now be wholly abandoned, and I plodded on, mostly by night, till I stood by Balin's tomb in Moria. There I halted for a long while.'[5] The artist *is* the hero, especially a medieval romance hero.

If so, then his editor and translator, like Sam, must serve as a kind of squire or yeoman to this knight. In prefaces to editions and translations of medieval works Tolkien performs such service by rendering the text accurately or translating the work faithfully. He refuses to interject any interpretation of the work that might interfere with the relationship between artist and reader and contribute to misunderstanding – he refuses to act like a critic. In the Preface to *Sir Gawain* he and E. V. Gordon stress the importance of reading the poem 'with an appreciation as far as possible of the sort which its author may be supposed to have desired'.[6] This goal may be attained by establishing a pure text with a full glossary that determines, 'as precisely as possible, the meaning of the author's actual words (in so far as the manuscript is fair to him)' (p. vii). In the Prefatory Note to the edition of the Corpus Manuscript of the *Ancrene Wisse* he explains with a minimum of critical fuss only those editorial notations necessary for the reader's benefit (retention of manuscript punctuation, changes in the treatment of abbreviations, acknowledgements, etc.).[7] Such self-effacement remains necessary because critical assertions may divert the reader from the poem itself, a warning presented in the Preface to the *Sir Gawain* edition:

Much of the literature that begins to gather about *Sir Gawain and the Green Knight*, though not without interest, has little bearing on this object, and many of the theories held, or questions asked, about the poem have here been passed over or lightly handled – the nature and significance of the 'test': the sources, near and remote, of the story's elements and details; the identity, character, life and other writings of the author (who remains unknown); his immediate motive in writing this romance; and so on.[8]

Translations in this light become more problematic because of the danger of misreading and thereby incorrectly translating the text; the possibility of subverting the reader – and the artist – increases. Thus the first task of the translator must be the ascertainment of meaning in the original. In his Preface to the translation of *Sir Gawain and the Green Knight* he declares that 'a translator must first try to discover as precisely as he can what his original means, and may be led by ever closer attention to understand it better for its own sake' (p. 7). Tolkien applauds M. B. Salu's translation of the Corpus Manuscript of the *Ancrene Wisse* in a preface that certifies the authenticity of the manuscript used in the translation, its value for the translator and reader (few scribal alterations because of his familiarity with the language ensure the possibility that the original intention of the artist will be preserved in this translation), and the success of the translation in rendering into modern idiom that mixture of 'cultivated speech' and 'colloquial liveliness' characteristic of its author.[9] The translator does not compete with the artist but collaborates; in this manner, valuable works in unknown languages can be given continuing 'life', as is *The Pearl* in Tolkien's posthumously published translation which is justified in the preface because '*The Pearl* certainly deserves to be heard by lovers of English poetry who have not the opportunity or the desire to master its difficult idiom' (p. 7).

Yet earlier, in the 1940 Prefatory Remarks to the Clark Hall translation of *Beowulf*, Tolkien cautions that no translation is 'offered as a means of judging the original, or as a substitute for reading the poem itself',[10] especially if the poem, like *Beowulf*, is 'a work of skilled and close-wrought metre' (p. ix). Such a translation helps a student only by providing 'an exercise for correction' rather than 'a model for imitation' (p. xvi). If a student does not return to the original he risks misunderstanding and even disliking the poem, like the critic who condemned *Beowulf* as 'only small beer' because he had used an incompetent translation (p. ix). Thus while a 'translation may be a useful form of commentary' on the poem, as Tolkien admits in the preface to his *Pearl*-Poet translations (p. 7), it still remains a commentary by the critic and not necessarily by the artist, and can become an act of presumption: Tolkien confesses that his own continued close study of poems like *Sir Gawain*, *Pearl*, and *Sir Orfeo* allowed him to learn more about them 'than I knew when I first *presumed* to translate them' (p. 7, my italics).

Although Tolkien's editions and translations attempt to render the original as closely as possible with the greatest respect for the artist and his work of art, his early critical and scholarly articles seem to ignore the literary merits of the medieval work under discussion and focus on its philological and historical features. In the 1929 essay on '*Ancrene Wisse* and *Hali Meiðhad*' Tolkien confesses rather defensively that 'my interest in this document [*Ancrene Wisse*] is linguistic'.[11] Like the 'translator' of *Farmer Giles* he disparages the literary interests of other students of the work and defends his decision to focus on its extra-literary features: 'it is very possible that nothing I can say about it will be either new or illuminating to the industrious or leisured that have kept up with it [literature surrounding the *Ancrene Wisse*]. I have not' (p. 104). A linguist here like some of the scholars lambasted by Tolkien in the *Beowulf* article, he is also an analyst of sources and influences in the Introduction to his translations of two of the *Pearl* Poet's poems and *Sir Orfeo*, where he reveals that research into the sources of *Sir Gawain* 'interests me' although 'it interested educated men of the fourteenth century very little' (p. 17). In short, Tolkien perfectly fulfils the role of the critic he so cleverly denigrates in the *Beowulf* and fairy-story lectures (themselves, by the way, for all their support of the creative process and art-for-art's-sake, as critical and interpretive as any work of literary criticism).

Tolkien displays a self divided by two different interests, art and philology and literary criticism, which tug him first one way, then another. Such a split self emerges in all three of his mock prefaces to creative works – one by an 'editor' in *The Adventures of Tom Bombadil*, one by a 'translator' in *Farmer Giles of Ham*, and one by an 'artist' in *The Lord of the Rings*. The 'editor' of hobbit songs by Bilbo, Sam, and their descendants in the first preface not only traces the chronology of the songs (based on historical evidence from the trilogy) and notes linguistic peculiarities of these songs as would any editor (in particular, strange words and rhyming and metrical tricks absorbed from the elves), but in addition as a literary critic he denigrates individual songs: '. . . some are written carelessly in margins and blank spaces. Of the last sort most are nonsense, now often unintelligible even when legible, or half-remembered fragments.'[12] By stressing the value of these songs *only* as historical and linguistic documents, the 'editor' uses the poems as a means to his own end. That this 'editor' is actually the artist himself symbolises the concept of the split self which also appears in *Farmer Giles of Ham* with greater subtlety. The critic here is a 'translator' rather than an editor, and hence capable of even greater acts of presumption against the artist's tale, as we have seen previously. Throughout his preface he makes mistakes in his scholarship which undermine his authority and reveal his human flaws. When this supposed historian analyses the character of the age with which the Latin work deals, he says that his information comes from 'historians of the reign of Arthur', presumably from a 'sober annal'; but in fact he paraphrases a 'popular lay' by the artist at whom he scoffs throughout. Compare his remarks that, 'What with the love of petty independence on the one hand, and on the other the greed of kings for wider realms, the years were filled with swift alternations of war and peace, of mirth and woe' (p. 7), with Tolkien's translation of the introductory lines of *Sir Gawain and the Green Knight*: 'where strange things, strife and sadness, / at whiles in the land did fare, / and each other grief and gladness / oft fast have followed there' (p. 25). A plagiarist like many medieval artists, ironically this 'translator' also functions like the modern literary critic he reproaches when he unknowingly disparages Aeneas, the lord of 'well-nigh all the wealth in the Western Isles' in *Sir Gawain*, by attributing the instability of the years to 'the greed of kings for wider realms'. His inaccuracies and self-deceptions transcend the useful if unfactual fancies of the artist: he becomes a mirror-image of the artist he denigrates. When he attempts to undercut the false fiction and the pride of his medieval artist ('the original grandiose title has been suitably reduced to *Farmer Giles of Ham*,' p. 8), his own falsity and pride are themselves undercut by the real artist, Tolkien, in this superb satire. The humble vernacular title and the crude subject matter ascribed to this 'curious tale' reflect not only the true character of the artist but also that of the critic. Both actually project the two sides of Tolkien.

In his own Foreword to *The Lord of the Rings* the artist and the critic initially seem to alternate voices, first one addressing the reader, then the other. Professor Tolkien the Historian in the Appendices and Prologue to *The Lord of the Rings* acts like an Andrew Lang in collecting, classifying, and organising historical and philological information about a non-existent species and world – but ones created by J. R. R. Tolkien the Artist. Such a mask enhances the verisimilitude of the secondary world of Middle-earth, very like the mask of Gulliver provided by Swift in the preface to *Gulliver's Travels* as a kind of passport authenticating the travels of the central hero. In this case, because there are two 'masks', the Artist and Critic clash dramatically with one another or battle as do hero and monstrous adversary in *Beowulf*. If the Artist in his creative travails may be described as a hobbit-like romance hero on a journey-quest to the Crack of Doom, then the Critic in his interruptions of the Artist's work may be described as a Sauron-like monster jeopardising the quest. Initially the man who became a professor of Old English and the man who became an artist were the same. Just as Tolkien the man in the primary world became attracted to an earlier age – the Middle Ages – instead of finding interest in the twentieth century, so Tolkien the sub-creator in the secondary world became attracted to its earlier age: of *The Lord of the Rings* Tolkien confesses that 'the story was drawn irresistibly towards the older world, and became an account, as it were, of its end and passing away before its beginning and middle had been told' (p. viii). The problem in both worlds is that the Sauron-like Critic or Scholar in Tolkien interferes with artistic progress – a moving *forward* on the quest for completion. In the primary world the teaching and research of Professor Tolkien prevented much artistic progress on the sequel during the years 1936–45.[13] In the secondary world creation halted altogether after the completion of *The Hobbit* while Tolkien the philologist attempted to complete the mythology and legends of the Elder Days, although 'I had little hope that other people would be interested in this work, especially since it was primarily *linguistic* in inspiration and was begun in order to provide the necessary background of *"history"* for Elvish tongues' (p. viii, my italics).

   In the Foreword his critical voice insists on analysing very rationally the artistry of *The Lord of the Rings* in opposition to the simple, humble, and emotional Artist's voice that refers the reader to the text itself rather than to any critical assertions. For example, the Critic asseverates that the events taking place in the primary world, specifically the Second World War, had no impact on those in the secondary world of the trilogy – 'If it had inspired or directed the development of the legend, then certainly the Ring would have been seized and used against Sauron; he would not have been annihilated but enslaved' (p.x). Certainly the fantasy with its secondary world boasts a happy ending alien to the reality of the primary world, but that does not mean the artist can protect the secondary world he creates from any contamination by the primary world. The Critic's voice seems to grow more shrill, more dictatorial:

> . . . it has been supposed by some that 'The Scouring of the Shire' reflects the situation in England at the time when I was finishing my tale. *It does not*. It is an essential part of the plot, foreseen from the outset, though in the event modified by the character of Saruman as developed in the story *without, need I say, any allegorical significance or contemporary political reference whatsoever*. (p. xi, my italics)

This voice of the rational man so concerned with truth warns the reader not to 'define the process' wherein an author is affected by his own experience because such hypotheses constitute mere 'guesses from evidence that is inadequate and ambiguous' (p. xi). Yet on the same page Tolkien quietly reveals that 'By 1918 all but one of my close friends were dead' (p. xi) – as a consequence of the First World War instead of the Second, true, but also a fact that startles and moves the reader. While the Critic may reject haphazard guesses about the artist's life and its relation to his work because of inadequate evidence, the Artist elicits directly the irrational, speculative, imaginative response from his reader. The latter is the same speaker who wishes to 'try his hand at a really long story that would hold the attention of readers, amuse them, delight them, and at times maybe excite them or deeply move them' (p. ix), no doubt as we are moved by the revelation about the loss of youthful friends in the war. Like the *Beowulf* poem portrayed as a medieval hero in the first *exemplum* of the article, the Artist relies on the godfather Poesis that Beowulf's false allegorical guides spurn: 'As a guide I had only my own *feelings* for what is appealing or moving' (p. ix, my italics).

The conflict between the two voices intensifies with the reader caught in the middle, for the Critic adopts the mask of the Artist in order to sway the reader, and in a sense triumphs over the Artist. He announces that *The Lord of the Rings* cannot be allegory, first because 'I cordially dislike allegory in all its manifestations', second because 'I think that many confuse "applicability" with "allegory" ', and third because 'the one resides in the freedom of the reader, and the other in the purposed domination of the author' (p. xi). It is ironic then that Tolkien as Artist has employed an allegory when he compares his labours to those of Frodo the quest-hero; he has as well confessed his domination by the *Critic* during the years 1939–45. It is perhaps a similar domination by this Critic which forces the *persona* to announce that '. . . this paperback edition and no other has been published with my consent and co-operation. Those who approve of courtesy (at least) to living authors will purchase it and no other' (p. xiii). Of course in the primary world Tolkien the man suffered from the unauthorised publication of the trilogy by Ace Books, but in this fictional projection of the 'drama' of the real or primary world, the heroic Artist has been overcome by the monstrous avarice of the Critic. Tolkien behind the mask of his *persona* wishes to alert the reader to a key theme of *The Lord of the Rings* without actually saying so. He does this in a very clever way.

At the end of his long and difficult journey-quest Frodo suddenly refuses to relinquish the Ring to the flame – he clings Gollum-like to his Precious. He has been affected by his long possession of this material object created by the Dark Lord, and it makes him selfish. Similarly at the end of *his* quest in the Foreword, the Artist succumbs to *his* dark side, of which the Critic is an emblem, and in a sense refuses to give up *his* own creation: 'Nonetheless, for all its defects of omission and inclusion, [*The Lord of the Rings*] was the product of long labour, and like a simple-minded hobbit I feel that it is, while I am still alive, my property in justice unaffected by copyright laws' (p. xii). As a hobbit he accordingly compares the pirate publisher to 'Saruman in his decay'. In the secondary world of the fantasy, Gollum unintentionally saves the fallen hobbit from himself by biting off his ring-finger and forcing him to give up that Ring he loves most in an act that also saves Middle-earth. But who saves the fallen artist in the primary world? As Tolkien the Critic noted, the Ring would never have been destroyed in the real world, hence the fallen artist might never be saved. Perhaps the Critic saves the Artist from himself by biting off *his* ring-finger: by interpreting the trilogy

specifically as non-allegory, he alerts the reader to possible 'purposed domination' by the *Critic* in the Foreword and forces him to
read the text more carefully to see if it is indeed allegorical. (That is,
just as the author may guide the reader's response by creating an
allegory, as Tolkien has in the Foreword, so the critic may guide his
response by claiming it is *not* an allegory.) Fortunately, the reader's
quest does not end on the last page of the Foreword when the
artist-hobbit seems to succumb to his own greed, nor at the end of
the Ring's life at the Crack of Doom in the trilogy when the
hero-hobbit succumbs to *his* greed, but instead at the end of *The
Lord of the Rings* when the servant-hobbit Sam returns to the Shire
and announces simply, in the last words of the work, 'Well, I'm
back.' The real hero spurns the Ring out of love for and obedience
to his master Frodo and demands neither 'courtesy' nor 'payment'
because unlike fallen man he suffers neither the sin of pride nor of
avarice. In this secondary world the innocent artist in Tolkien can
also come 'back' like Sam and be reborn as the author of hobbit-
song. At the end of his own journey-quest the reader realises the
Artist has triumphed over the Critic at last.

As a Frodo-like hobbit on the way to Mount Doom the reader
must exercise his own free will when tempted by others such as the
Dark Lord and Gandalf, or the Critic, to guide his responses when
he puts on the Ring (that is, when he reads *The Lord of the Rings*).
Only he can decide for himself whether the work has 'inner
meaning', despite the Critic's proclamation that 'it has in the
intention of the author none. It is neither allegorical nor topical' (p.
x). By so doing he helps to rescue the Artist from the Critic.

That the Artist and Critic may be the same figure in the dramatic
Foreword or the same man in the real world is an idea rehearsed
for Tolkien in *Beowulf*, where the hero Beowulf never fully realises
his most awesome adversary is the monster of pride within
himself, and by Tolkien in the Beowulf essay in which the critic
never fully realises he himself is a monster like the irrelevant
monsters he ignores. Many of these ideas derive from the Christian
culture imbuing those medieval works of literature Tolkien loved
and studied all his life.

III God's Word: Satan as Critic

For Tolkien, the critic figure based upon the monster Grendel or
the Dragon typifies Satan, as the artist figure based upon the hero

Beowulf typifies the Creator. This myth of literary roles springs from the book of Genesis as a preface or foreword to the Word of God and the book of Revelation, the 'rising' and 'setting' aspects of the Bible related to the 'rising' and 'setting' moments and balanced structure of *Beowulf*. Paradoxically the rising of the first book actually involves a fall – of man – as the setting of the last book involves his rising – or redemption. Because of the Fall instigated by Satan, man suffers a split self, with one side a monster and one side a hero – one side a child and one side an adult ('growing up' is necessary only in a world subjected to mutability, sickness, and death, all consequences of the Fall). So divided, man longs for an other world where he may be whole. This world he experiences only briefly on earth when a godlike sub-creator fashions a secondary world analogous to the Other World. In this secondary world of art, the word like the Word of God (the Bible, especially Revelation), provides redemption ('recovery' through joy) for the world-weary fallen adult. Unfortunately the critic attempts to interfere by guiding the reader away from fantasy and literature toward drama, a form that mirrors the reality and sorrow of the primary world, just as Satan tries to lure man away from the eternal good of the Other World by offering him the temporal good of this world. He also tries to dominate the free will of the reader by imposing on him his own interpretation of that literature or drama. This myth Tolkien constructs in the two lectures, his 'Genesis' and 'Revelation', and applies in the Foreword to *The Lord of the Rings* in particular.

The concept of Satan as critic first surfaces in the *Beowulf* article. As God in Genesis first creates Eden as a paradise arousing Satan's envy, so in *Beowulf*, Tolkien notes, the artist as tower-builder (Hrothgar) constructs Heorot so that 'its light spread over many lands' ('lixte se leoma ofer landa fela') in parody of 'fiat lux' in Genesis, arousing the envy of the monster Grendel: 'Grendel is maddened by the sound of harps' (p. 88). This music signals the peace and joy of community denied to that exile suffering the mark of Cain. Grendel is the critic of light as Hrothgar and the scop are its artists: 'the outer darkness and its hostile offspring lie ever in wait for the torches to fail and the voices to cease' (p. 88). Similarly the human *Beowulf*-critic arrogantly tries to muffle the artist's voice by using the poem as a means to an end – as a demonstration of his superior understanding of Old English history and linguistics. Preferring knowledge to wisdom, he resembles the monstrous

serpent who tempts Eve with the desire to be Godlike by eating of
the Tree of Knowledge of Good and Evil. Such knowledge is
pursued in *The Lord of the Rings*, for example, by Saruman, the
perverted wizard (teacher? sage?) who gazes myopically into the
palantir (ironically meaning 'farsighted') in a vain attempt to boost
his own knowledge and power and to emulate the Dark Lord
Sauron. He exchanges for his previous wisdom mere knowledge
('all those arts and subtle devices, for which he forsook his former
wisdom'), never realising those 'which fondly he imagined were
his own, came but from Mordor'.[14] Appropriately he inhabits the
citadel named Orthanc, 'Cunning Mind' in the language of the
Mark but in Elvish the monstrous name 'Mount Fang', to underscore the exact nature of his perversion or 'fall'. (Even Sauron
originally misused elven wisdom in creating the rings as a means
to the end of self-aggrandisement.) Saruman like the wily serpent
of Eden uses his own voice to dissuade others from courses of
action not beneficial to him, literally when challenged by Gandalf
and his followers on the steps of Orthanc, but more figuratively
through his surrogate voice, 'Worm*tongue*', when his evil counsel
demoralises Theoden in the hall of Rohan. Significantly by the end
of the trilogy Saruman has become 'Sharkey' and Wormtongue his
beast 'Worm', both names connoting the cold-blooded and animal
nature of the monster.

To the portrait of Satan as a critic of the creation God's work,
Tolkien adds the portrait of Christ as its heroic defender – the
Word of God, or the archetype of the human artist – in the pair of
works, 'On Fairy Stories' and 'Leaf by Niggle', comprising *Tree and
Leaf*. He even mentions the Fall in the former through the 'Locked
Door' theme: 'Even Peter Rabbit was forbidden a garden, lost his
blue coat, and took sick. The Locked Door stands as an eternal
temptation' (p. 33). The critic longs to explore the 'Tree of Tales' –
like the Tree of Knowledge of Good and Evil – with its 'intricately
knotted and ramified *history* of the branches' related to the
philologist's study of the 'tangled skein of *language*' (p. 19, my
italics). Unlike the critic, the artist Niggle in 'Leaf by Niggle'
merely wishes to portray accurately a single leaf. The humble,
self-effacing, and imaginative artist contrasts with the proud,
ambitious, and analytic Critic. This is one reason why Tolkien
dramatically combines the analytic and ambitious prose essay of
the critic, 'On Fairy Stories', with the humble, self-effacing, and
imaginative prose tale of the artist, 'Leaf by Niggle', in one volume

– *Tree and Leaf*. Its title[15] appropriately mirrors the mythic difference between the two media and roles. For there were two trees in
Eden, the Tree of Knowledge of Good and Evil and the Tree of
Life. The wood of the latter was used for the cross upon which
Christ was crucified to redeem man. And 'Leaf by Niggle', as
Tolkien explains in the Introductory Note to *Tree and Leaf*, was
inspired by the felling of a great tree by its owner, 'a punishment
for any crimes it may have been accused of, such as being large and
alive' (p. 2). The tree destroyed wantonly by its equally fallen
owner in our fallen world suggests the loss of the Tree of Life, a
metonymy for Eden, by its gardener Adam.[16] It implies as well its
resurrection as a 'leaf' by the artist Niggle (or as 'Leaf by Niggle' by
the artist Tolkien), who eventually creates or restores a whole tree,
then a 'sub-creation' or another world. This is the Tree of Life, a
metonymy for the paradise Niggle is permitted to inhabit eternally
by the story's end.

The distinction between the two Trees and between Satan and
Christ was amplified in the Middle Ages to include as well a
distinction between the Old Man and the New Man or the child, a
typology Tolkien also uses in 'On Fairy-Stories' to distinguish the
adult-critic from the child-reader. For example, in the *Cursor
Mundi* Christ the Second Adam rests as a new-born child on the
top of a faded tree (the Tree of Knowledge around which an adder
is wrapped) reaching to the sky, at whose roots is buried Abel,
slain by Cain who resides in Hell.[17] This image of the *novus homo*
underscores the idea of rebirth and spiritual regeneration, which St
Augustine in *De Doctrina Christiana* asks us to put on like a snake
wriggling out of its skin in place of the *vetus homo*, the Old Man. He
means that we should exchange the life of the senses, of the body,
of the Old Law, for the life of the spirit, of the soul, of the New Law
of Christianity.[18] Interestingly, Tolkien as critic refers pejoratively
to himself as an 'old man' in the Foreword to *The Lord of the Rings*: 'I
cordially dislike allegory in all its manifestations, and always have
done so since I grew *old and wary enough* to detect its presence' (p.
xi, my italics). That Tolkien's old critic was meant to embody St
Augustine's Old Man becomes more convincing within the context
of the same passage, wherein St Augustine also blames the Old
Man for adhering to the letter in reading the Bible instead of
preferring the spirit, or an understanding of figurative signs and
expressions of allegory. Throughout Tolkien's works oldness is
linked with literalness and knowledge as an end in itself. First, like

this Old Man, Tolkien's Critic in the Foreword prefers 'history, true or feigned, with its varied applicability to the thought and experience of readers' (p. xi) to allegory. Second, Tolkien also condemns the Old Man or the adult in his essay, 'On Fairy-Stories', whereas he glorifies that symbolic child or New Man in each human being still able to receive 'grace' – to be transported by the 'word' of the sub-creator to the other world of Faërie where he experiences the eucatastrophe of the happy ending of fantasy. He does caution that 'The process of growing older is not necessarily allied to growing wickeder, though the two do often happen together' (p. 44). Finally, in *The Lord of the Rings* the old and wary Saruman disintegrates into dust at death whereas the aged Gandalf, his good counterpart, dies as the Grey (puts off the Old Man) so as to be reborn as the White (puts on the New Man).

The New Man as the archetype of Christ symbolises the incarnation of the Word of God in human form, a divine communication by the penultimate artist, God, to his 'reader', fallen or Old Man, a metaphor made explicit by St Augustine:

How did He come except that 'the Word was made flesh, and dwelt among us'? It is as when we speak. In order that what we are thinking may reach the mind of the listener through the fleshy ears, that which we have in mind is expressed in words . . . by means of which it may reach the ears without suffering any deterioration in itself. In the same way the Word of God was made flesh without change that He might dwell among us. (1.13, p. 14)

Elsewhere in *De Doctrina* St Augustine reveals that the often allegorical Word of God is incarnated in the 'flesh' of parable[19] as is perfect love and truth in Christ the Word. This Word corresponds to the word of man, especially when the latter communicates the truth hidden in that parabolic Word eloquently and clearly by using the tropes, styles, and rules of rhetoric. Man discerns the truth by applying the four-fold allegorical method of exegesis to the text.

Although Tolkien's Critic in the Foreword cannot abide allegory, a sign of his 'oldness', Tolkien himself in the *Beowulf* article associates allegory as distinct from myth with that abstraction and rational analysis of which the critic rather than the artist is fond. Further, the bad artist in both the Foreword and the *Beowulf* article is accused of dominating the reader by using allegory instead of myth. This does not mean Tolkien dislikes figurative expression, of which allegory is one kind. Indeed, he constructs the central fantasy of the *Beowulf* article through the use of figurative expressions – allegorical and metaphorical *exempla*. Defining allegory very narrowly, he notes that *The Pearl*, for example, is not an allegory but *is* allegorical, a differentiation hotly debated by *Pearl* critics in the past.[20] Allegory must be confined (as Tolkien reveals in the Introduction to his translation of *The Pearl*) to

> narrative, to an account (however short) of events; and symbolism to the use of visible signs of things to represent other things or ideas. . . . To be an 'allegory' a poem must *as a whole*, and with fair consistency, describe in other terms some event or process; its entire narrative and all its significant details should cohere and work together to make the end. . . . But an allegorical description of an event does not make that event itself allegorical. (p. 18)

This distinction between symbolism and allegory remains a modern one; St Augustine would not have quarrelled with Tolkien. Note also that Tolkien's fellow Inkling C. S. Lewis knew of his friend's dislike of allegory but preferred to define the word in a wider sense:

> I am also convinced that the wit of man *cannot* devise a story in wh. the wit of some other man cannot find an allegory. . . . Indeed, in so far as the things unseen are manifested by the things seen, one might from one point of view call the whole material universe an allegory. . . . It wd. be disastrous if anyone took your statement that the Nativity is the greatest of all allegories to mean that the physical event was merely *feigned*.[21]

It is interesting to note that Tolkien's conception of the secondary world created by the artist in his fantasy depends upon allegory: the art of man corresponds to the art of God and the secondary world of Faërie resembles the other world of Heaven. In 'On Fairy-Stories' Tolkien shows that the process of reading a fantasy imitates the process of reading (and living by) the Word of God. The Christian experiences joy in 'reading' the happy ending or eucatastrophe of man's history in the birth of Christ as he enjoys

the 'happy ending' of the story of the Incarnation in the Resurrection. Similarly he 'escapes' from this world into the 'secondary
world' of fantasy to experience as a child the joy of Recovery, as the
Christian escapes from this world after death into the other world
of Heaven to experience as a child eternal joy: for the Christian, life
with its happy ending is a Divine Comedy, as Dante shrewdly
noted. This message is imparted to the grieving father of *The Pearl*
in a dream in which he confronts his lost child (or soul), after
which his spirits are themselves lifted in a Happy Ending which
invokes Revelation. It is a work Tolkien chose appropriately to
translate into modern English. The child must be the *novus homo* or
the New Man, a type of Christ, who is lost and then found by the
old man, the father, as a type of Adam.

Art then heals the split in the self by renewing fallen man. Just as
the Old Man puts on the New Man, so the adult regains the child
by reading fantasy and the critic becomes the artist, by creating it,
as Tolkien himself did. Unfortunately in the primary world man is
neither wholly one nor the other; he remains both. A metaphor for
the loss of unified sensibility caused by the Fall, the split self or the
antithetical pair reflects that rivalry between the sons of Adam,
Abel and Cain, which results in fratricide, the archetype of the
murder of Deagol by Smeagol and the symbol of the quality of
existence in the land ruled by Sauron, Mordor or Morðor, the
Anglo-Saxon word for murder. The split self and the pair link
many of Tolkien's fictional characters: Tidwald the old churl argues
with the young minstrel Torhthelm in 'The Homecoming of
Beorhtnoth Beorhthelm's Son'; Niggle the artist is irritated by his
neighbour Parish the gardener in 'Leaf by Niggle'; Alf the humble
apprentice serves Nokes the arrogant Master Cook in 'Smith of
Wootton Major; and of course Theoden and Denethor rule as good
and evil leaders, opposites like Denethor's good and evil sons,
Faramir and Boromir, in *The Lord of the Rings.* The divided self of
Bilbo, half Baggins, half Took, cannot decide whether to act as a
grocer or a burglar in *The Hobbit,* just as Gollum argues with his
other self, Smeagol, in the trilogy.

Within the context of medieval Christianity then, the split self
constitutes a badge of man's fallen nature as both good and evil.
But this favourite theme of Tolkien's art finds other contexts: in
that of medieval literature, the conflict can be sketched as a
Germanic heroic battle which can also be interpreted as a Christian
allegory. Within the context of twentieth-century literary history in

the twenties and thirties, the conflict projects the support of one school of artists for the art-for-art's-sake movement and one school of literary critics for the New Criticism in reaction to the nineteenth-century view of art and criticism as socially, historically, linguistically, culturally useful, both views Germanic in nature.[22] Within the context of the 'history' of his own life, the war between the critic and the artist or the professor of Anglo-Saxon and the Christian reflects antithetical interests never completely reconciled[23] except in the fantasy world of his art, where the critic is redeemed by the artist and the best warrior is the most sacrificial and gentle. So *Beowulf*, a poem Tolkien greatly loved that depicted clashes between Germanic and Christian values, battles between hero and monsters, and a contrast between the 'rising' and 'setting' moments of the protagonist's life, remains amazingly and joyfully a single, unified, and balanced poem.

2 The King under the Mountain: Tolkien's Children's Story

A story about growing up or maturation, *The Hobbit* has been regarded by some critics as merely a work of children's literature,[1] or else as a badly-muddled mixture of children's literature and adult literature.[2] While critical interpretations have revealed the psychological and literary underpinnings of the adult level of the work,[3] they rarely justify or even account for the children's level – specifically, the existence of the narrator and the children's story framework. Tolkien himself has admitted that his own children disliked the tone and style in which it was written:

> 'The Hobbit' was written in what I should now regard as bad style, as if one were talking to children. There's nothing my children loathed more. They taught me a lesson. Anything that was in any way marked out in 'The Hobbit' as for children, instead of just for people, they disliked – instinctively. I did too, now that I think about it.[4]

The reason that Tolkien employed the children's story apparatus that offended even his own children has to do with the *adult* level of the work: his narrative technique constitutes part of the work's fiction, in the manner of Chaucer's *Canterbury Tales*. The narrator, like a tale-telling pilgrim, must be regarded as one additional character.

The arrogant, unimaginative, and very 'adult' narrator assumes this story about little hobbits must be relegated to an audience of little creatures – children. His literalism betrays his 'oldness' in the Augustinian sense. For in the 1938 Andrew Lang Lecture on fairy-stories Tolkien indicates that fantasy appeals to the child in every adult. So *The Hobbit* is a children's story only in this sense; otherwise it is a genre as fictional and false as *The Hobbit*'s narrator. As a critic who denies the artist's intention by misunderstanding the story and its characters, the narrator also personifies the critic whom Tolkien views as a monster in the *Beowulf* essay and against whom Tolkien, as heroic defender of the poem as a work of art, must battle.

In this seminal essay in which Tolkien explains how he reads *Beowulf* there are many other ideas and concepts he fictionalises in *The Hobbit*, although critics have not generally recognised this.[5] The lecture was published as an article one year before *The Hobbit* of 1937.[6] In it, as we have seen, Tolkien revolutionised *Beowulf* scholarship by interpreting its previously ignored monsters as central thematically and structurally to the meaning of the poem; in addition he poked fun at the critical 'monsters' – the scholars – who had dismissed it as a work of art in their eagerness to trumpet its historical, philological, and anthropological importance. The monsters Grendel and the Dragon were for Tolkien not only fierce enemies of the Danes and Geats against whom Beowulf fought, but also, in a more symbolic fashion, projections of spiritual and political flaws in Beowulf himself. Aged and yet still boasting of his youthful prowess in battle, King Beowulf fights the Dragon in an ill-advised move that will result in his death and the betrayal of his people, for the Swedes among other tribes will attack the leaderless Geats after he dies. He manifests that same pride in his own ability and greed for dragon-gold as the Dragon, and although he wins the battle with the monster (with the help of Wiglaf) he loses the one with himself. 'For it is true of man, maker of myths,' Tolkien declares, 'that Grendel and the Dragon, in their lust, greed, and malice, have a part in him.'[7]

Tolkien's ideas about kingship in *Beowulf*, which he also employed in *The Hobbit*, were perhaps influenced by a scholarly study of the poem published in 1929 by Levin L. Schücking on 'The Ideal of Kingship in *Beowulf*'.[8] More generally they find expression in the thirteenth-century *Ancrene Wisse*, 'Guide for Anchoresses', a work which first captured Tolkien's interest in a 1929 linguistic study and later in the preface to a translation in 1956 (of which he approved) and in his own critical edition of 1962.[9] Schücking cites St Augustine to define the true and wise king and his antithesis, the false and tyrannical king.

> In contrast to such a 'rex justus' ['just king'] who always appears as a *good shepherd* and with the *qualities of a father*, is the 'tyrannus' or 'rex iniustus,' who is ruled by the 'radix vitiorum' ['root of vices'], 'superbia' ['pride'] or 'amor sui' ['love of self'] . . . Out of *amor sui* spring all other vices, such as 'invidia, ira, tristitia, avaritia, and ventris ingluvies' ['envy, wrath, sadness, avarice and gluttony']. (p. 39)

The vices of the bad king can be recognised as four of the seven deadly sins. These sins assume the shape of animals and monsters in the *Ancrene Wisse*; wild beasts inhabit the wilderness we must all travel on the way to the Heavenly Jerusalem, or the Kingdom of the Elect.

> But go with great caution, for in this wilderness there are many evil beasts: the Lion of Pride, the Serpent of venomous Envy, the Unicorn of Wrath, the Bear of deadly Sloth, the Fox of Covetousness, the Sow of Gluttony, the Scorpion with its tail of stinging lechery, that is, Lust. These, listed in order, are the Seven Deadly Sins. (p. 86)

The connection between the sinful king and the monster in *Beowulf*, St Augustine, and the *Ancrene Wisse* reappears in *The Hobbit*. Tolkien calls his dragon Smaug 'King under the Mountain' because under a mountain he guards a treasure which he wrongfully stole from previous dwarf-kings. The epithet serves to link this inhuman monster with similar monsters – and monstrous kings or leaders – elsewhere in *The Hobbit* through four major significations. First, it refers to the monsters of the work as a whole: Smaug guards his treasure under the Lonely Mountain while Gollum hides his magic ring under the Misty Mountains. In addition there are other monsters like the trolls, goblins, wargs, and giant spiders. Second, there also exist elf, human, dwarf, and hobbit 'kings' or leaders who, like Beowulf, succumb to various monstrous vices, chiefly pride and greed. These include the Elvenking, the Master of Dale, the dwarf-king Thorin, and even

Bilbo, who rules Bag End located in *Underhill*, Hobbiton. Third, it symbolises the position of the narrator who dominates the narrative through his frequent, usually critical, interjections intended to undermine the artist's tale. Finally, the phrase suggests the children's game of 'King of the Mountain' in which various combatants try to topple a hill's resident 'king'. It appropriately evokes the children's level of the novel used by Tolkien to mask his more serious purpose.

Furthermore, the Augustinian and Stoic-Christian idea of the good prince which Schücking sees in the Germanic and heroic Old English *Beowulf* resurfaces in the modern English *Hobbit*. Eventually Bilbo develops into a type of the good 'king' when he tests his courage, justice, prudence (wisdom and intelligence but also awareness of moral good), and finally temperance or *mensura* (the bridling of emotions by moderation) in battles with those monsters. For Schücking an exemplar of such an Augustinian king occurs in Beowulf, as when he humbly and wisely refuses the crown offered by Hygd 'in favour of his relation; thus, he becomes a member of the virtuous society which supports the ideal of temperance' (p. 48). But Tolkien as we have seen perceives Beowulf, and hence Bilbo, whom he models in part upon this king, as more flawed and monstrous than does Schücking. For him the ultimate model of the good king that Bilbo must become, after vanquishing his internal monsters of the deadly sins of pride and greed, is Christ. This king's monstrous adversary is the Devil, whose role in perverting man from good is 'to incite us to the venomous vices such as pride, disdain, envy, and anger, and to their venomous offspring', according to the *Ancrene Wisse* (p. 85). In this same work Christ as a 'good shepherd' with the 'qualities of a father' is portrayed as a true and good king or knight of the Kingdom of the Elect. When the soul is attacked by demons and devils, Jesus proves his love and performs chivalric deeds in tournament play so that his shield (his body, which disguises his Godhead) is pierced on the cross. The parallel continues:

> . . . after the death of a brave knight, his shield is hung high in the church in his memory. And so is this shield, the crucifix, set in the church, where it may be most easily seen, that it may remind us of Jesus Christ's deed of knighthood on the cross. Let His beloved see by that how He bought her love, allowing his shield to be pierced, His side open, to show her His heart, to

show her own how completely He loved her, and to win her own heart. (p. 174)

His love for man surpasses the four kinds of human love – friendship, sexual love, mother-child love, and love between the body and the soul. It also suggests the love of God (*amor Dei*) that St Augustine contrasts with the self-love (*amor sui*) of the tyrant. It is this love that Bilbo emulates as he completes his spiritual maturation in the course of *The Hobbit* through the tests with the monsters.

The major difference, then, between Tolkien's conception of Beowulf in the essay and his conception of Bilbo in *The Hobbit* is Bilbo's success in combating literal and internal monsters and, at least for Tolkien, Beowulf's failure. In the two-part structure of *Beowulf* the hero clashes with two different monstrous adversaries, Grendel at the 'rising moment' of his life during his youth, and the Dragon at the 'setting moment', in his old age.[10] In the similarly structured *Hobbit* Bilbo battles with his two adversaries, Gollum and Smaug the dragon, at various *rising* moments only, for it is a story of spiritual maturation and not of spiritual death. This difference stems from the genres of the two works. Tolkien regards *Beowulf* explicitly as an elegy, defined as 'tragedy' in the 1938 Andrew Lang Lecture on fairy-stories because of its unhappy ending (dyscatastrophe) and hence its link with the primary world, and *The Hobbit* implicitly as a 'fantasy' because of its happy ending (eucatastrophe) and hence its link with the secondary world of sub-creation.[11] Their different genres affect the nature of the dual levels in each: the explicit Germanic-heroic ethic and culture of *Beowulf* masks a very Christian purpose, just as the explicit children's story framework of *The Hobbit* masks a more 'adult' and serious purpose.

We turn now to a closer examination of these ideas, beginning with the monsters in *The Hobbit*, turning next to Bilbo, and concluding with the narrator – all 'Kings under the Mountain'.

I The Monsters: Kings under the Mountain

If the balanced two-part structure of *The Hobbit* (Chapters 1–8 and 9–19) mirrors that of *Beowulf*, then its two parts must differ in emphasis because the two monsters differ. In the *Beowulf* lecture Tolkien explains: 'If the dragon is the right end for Beowulf, and I agree with the author that it is, then Grendel is an eminently suitable beginning. They are creatures, *feond mancynnes* [enemies of mankind], of a similar order and kindred significance. Triumph over the lesser and more nearly human is cancelled by defeat before the older and more elemental' (p. 86). In *The Hobbit*, Gollum, whose name begins with the same letter as Grendel's, assumes his place, and thus epitomises the 'lesser and more nearly human' vices as Smaug in the second part epitomises the 'older and more elemental' vices. It is the *Ancrene Wisse* which characterises the inward temptations as 'bodily in the case of lechery, gluttony, and sloth, spiritual in the case of pride, envy, and anger, and also of covetousness' (p. 85). The lesser sins are certainly the 'bodily' ones, which Gollum represents, just as Smaug represents the 'old and more elemental' spiritual ones.

Gollum, who enters the story in the middle (Chapter Five) of the first half (Chapters One to Eight), expresses 'bodily sin' chiefly through his perpetual hunger. Gluttonous even when young, he taught his own grandmother to suck eggs.[12] His name resembles the sound of swallowing associated with gulping food. Because his stomach remains in his mature years his sole concern he values himself above all, addressing himself as 'My Precious'. He represents that love of self (*amor sui*) specifically directed toward lower or bodily functions. The ring as a birthday present to himself symbolises the narcissism of the self turned too much inward. It produces an invisibility of self in the external world as if the self had been pushed one step past mere isolation into non-being.

This ring links Gollum with the dragon Smaug in the second part when Bilbo uses it to burgle the dragon's hoard of a cup, and it is this loss which arouses Smaug's anger (p. 208). But here the invisibility caused by the ring allows him to function as a better burglar: for Bilbo, the *alter ego* of the perverted hobbit Gollum, it symbolises that self-effacement requisite in loving one's neighbour for the sake of God. Thus he forgets his own fears, remembers the dwarves' mission, bravely steals the cup, and even tricks the dragon into revealing his vulnerable spot.

Smaug enters the story in the middle (Chapters Eleven to Thirteen) of the second part (Chapters Nine to Nineteen) and expresses 'spiritual sin' chiefly through his pride, although he also manifests wrath, avarice, and envy. After Bilbo has stolen his cup he nurses his avarice with the thought of revenge. Unfortunately, his pride leads to his fall. When Bilbo unctuously flatters him with the admission that 'I only wished to have a look at you and see if you were truly as great as tales say' (p. 212), Smaug begins showing off. He inadvertently reveals his vulnerable spot along with his diamond-studded underbelly while Bilbo exclaims, 'Dazzlingly marvellous' (p. 216). The dragon's avarice leads to his death, just as the *revelours'* search for the treasure leads to death in the *Pardoner's Tale*. 'Radix malorum est cupiditas', or avarice, as Chaucer's Pardoner tells it. Gold *is* death: in *The Hobbit* when the fools of Dale spot a heavenly light they assume the gold is on its way as legends had predicted and rush forward to – their deaths. For it is the fiery dragon himself, in a highly symbolic scene, who lights up the heavens.

The two monsters Gollum and Smaug are set apart from the other monsters by their isolation in central chapters. Nevertheless the adversary in the first part derives its essential nature from Gollum as the adversary in the second derives its essential nature from Smaug. The 'bodily sins' of gluttony and sloth (lechery omitted because this is a children's story) plus the sin of anger are portrayed in the monsters of the trolls, goblins, wargs, and giant insects and spiders. The more 'spiritual' sins of pride, envy, covetousness, and again anger are portrayed in the 'monsters' of the Elvenking, the Master of Dale, and the dwarf-king. In each part the hierarchy of monsters begins with the least dangerous and evil and climbs to the most dangerous and evil.

In the first part the trolls introduce the theme of gluttony in the appropriately-entitled chapter of 'Roast Mutton'. The mutton they roast on spits illustrates as well their laziness, for they actually detest it but are too lazy to seek out the 'manflesh' they prefer. When Bilbo's carelessness allows them to capture the hobbit and the dwarves, they quarrel angrily over the best cooking method for dwarf-flesh and forget that dawn is nigh. The coming of the sun turns them to stone as if to symbolise their spiritual numbness and 'death'. The goblins are the second monstrous adversary, encountered in Chapter Four, 'Over Hill and under Hill'. As interested in food as the trolls ('they are always hungry', p. 70), they even capture the dwarf ponies lodged in one of their caves. But they seem less civilised than the trolls, possibly because of their greater anger and sadism. They savagely flick whips as they herd the captured dwarves into the hall of the goblin-king and they build cruel machines of torture for innocent victims. The wargs of Chapter Six 'Out of the Frying Pan', resemble wolves in their shape and their brute anger. The night when they surround the

dwarves they intend to kill whole villages of woodmen except for a
few prisoners left alive for their goblin allies, merely because these
woodmen had encroached upon their forests. Finally the 'Flies and
Spiders' in Chapter Eight exemplify uncontrolled gluttony and
anger on the lowest level. After tying the dwarves up in trees, one
spider notes that 'the meat's alive and kicking' (p. 156). Their
gluttony is used by Bilbo to trick them: he lures them away from
the captured dwarves by describing himself as 'far more sweet
than other meat' (p. 158). He also invokes their anger. By calling
them insulting names like 'Attercop' and 'Tomnoddy' he makes
them so 'frightfully angry' that they follow the sound of his voice
while the invisible hobbit doubles back to untie the dwarves and
then battle with the returning, stupidly angry, giant pests.

The 'chain of evil being' traced in this first part is also used in the
second. In the first the trolls resemble Cockney-speaking humans,
followed by the goblins or orcs who pervert the species of elves,
the wolflike wargs, and on the least rational level, the insects and
spiders. In the second part the less physically dangerous 'monsters' threaten instead the various societies surrounding them
through their obsession with treasure and social position, in effect
revealing the flaws of avarice, envy, and pride. Hence they operate
behind the mask of the king or leader who occupies the highest
social and political position in the community. It is for this reason
that the chain of evil being in this part is one of individuals, rather
than of species as in the first part. It begins with the most noble
and least dangerous, the Elvenking, and progresses to the most
ignoble and dangerous, the dwarf-king Thorin, with man – the
Master of Dale – occupying a medial position. Interestingly, their
dwelling places reflect this hierarchy through their distance from
the earth – the elven treehouse, the human house, the dwarf hall
under the mountain.

The wood-elves and the men of Dale team up like the wargs and
goblins of the first part to fight the dwarves; both are inordinately
fond of gold. When the Elvenking 'strongly suspected attempted
burglary or something like it' from the dwarves (p. 192), he
imprisons them. The Master, less generously, 'believed they were
frauds who would sooner or later be discovered. . . . They were
expensive to keep, and their arrival had turned things into a long
holiday in which business was at a standstill' (p. 193). The
pragmatism of the Master reflects the concerns of trade and
business which preoccupy Dale, for in 'the great days of old . . .

they had been wealthy and powerful, and there had been fleets of boats on the waters' (p. 185). If the wood-elves with their king and ceremonious feasting function as an aristocracy, the men of Dale with their master and practical gatherings of townspeople function instead as a bourgeoisie. The lowest social class of criminals and thieves in one sense is comprised of the dwarves – but all of these kings and leaders spiritually, if not socially, betray an avarice and pride which groups them together as sinners. The Elvenking as a burglar steals the dwarves from Bilbo just as the Master of Dale as a fraud steals from his own people many years later. Each suspects the dwarves of that crime of which he and his people are most guilty.

Yet Thorin, king of the dwarves, does reveal most blatantly the sins of avarice and pride. He fulfils the predisposition of his people to such flaws: 'dwarves are not heroes, but calculating folk with a great idea of the value of money; some are tricky and treacherous and pretty bad lots; some are not, but are decent enough people like Thorin and Company, if you don't expect too much' (p. 204). Like the greedy dragon whose role as 'King under the Mountain' Thorin assumes after his death, he refuses to share the hoard with 'thieves' and 'enemies' such as the deserving men of Esgaroth or even his own comrade Bilbo: 'none of our gold shall thieves take or the violent carry off while we are alive!' (p. 245). In addition, his pride leads him into error. He ignores the wise raven Roäc who advises him that 'The treasure is likely to be your death, though the dragon is no more!' (p. 253). The treasure *is* his death. Indeed, he refuses to listen to anyone else but himself, although his apology to Bilbo at the moment of death rejuvenates him spiritually if not physically.

In a sense, the last 'King under the Mountain' is a legal trio introduced at the end of the novel. The tunnelling names of Grubb, Grubb, and Burrowes illustrate their literal and figurative positions as 'kings' or monsters under the mountain, in this case the 'very comfortable tunnel' belonging to Bilbo in *Underhill*. These dragon-like lawyers guard a treasure appropriately named *Bag* End which they intend to auction. A less frightening adversary than the others and therefore more easily overcome, nevertheless this hobbit trio forces Bilbo to realise that a 'King under the Mountain' may be a neighbour hobbit – or even oneself.

II Bilbo: Baggins of Underhill

At the very beginning of *The Hobbit* Bilbo acts as a 'King under the Mountain' when he hoards his wealth – food in the hobbit world – against depletion by strange intruding dwarves. Later he will describe himself as a foil for Smaug in a cryptic riddle: 'I come from under the hill, and under the hills and over the hills my paths led' (pp. 212–13). This 'King under the Mountain' must defeat himself before attempting to defeat other monsters, so that the real battle in *The Hobbit* might as well take place at home in the Shire. It is for this reason Tolkien subtitled the work 'There and Back Again', to draw attention to the geographical location of the major battle – not the Lonely Mountain, as a careless reader might assume, but 'There' – the Shire – and 'Back Again', as the first and last chapters precisely indicate.

In the first chapter, the dwarves and Gandalf arrive at the Shire to interrupt an irritable host for an 'Unexpected Party'; in the last chapter the dwarf Balin and Gandalf return to the Shire to interrupt a pleased host for a smaller but still unexpected party in 'The Last Stage'. It is Bilbo's attitude toward food which changes: at the beginning he complains to himself about the amount of food dwarves require, at the end he generously and unasked hands Gandalf the tobacco jar, laughing because he now realises the joy of community and the love of neighbour. For food provides not only physical sustenance and continued life but also on a higher level the renewal of spiritual life, as in the Christian Mass of the Eucharist. The absence of food, or the interruption of feasting, or the refusal to feast with others all communicate interference with the life-force, the life of the community, and symbolically spiritual life, or virtue. On the Germanic level, as in *Beowulf*, feasting celebrates the concern of warrior for warrior and lord. The raids on Heorot by Grendel symbolise the dark forces on earth against which man must fight to preserve his hall-joy and brotherhood. Tolkien describes the situation beautifully in the *Beowulf* essay: 'A light starts . . . and there is a sound of music; but the outer darkness and its hostile offspring lie ever in wait for the torches to fail and the voices to cease. Grendel is maddened by the sound of harps' (p. 88). Thus Bilbo's attitude toward the food used in feasting and the money used to buy that food becomes important in resolving his own inner conflicts and in battling against his monsters. The contrast between feasting and battle or the hero and the adversary is incorporated into *The Hobbit* in three ways: thematically through the confrontation between Bilbo and various monsters, structurally through an alternation of party chapters with battle chapters, and symbolically through the internalisation of the conflict within the hero.

Structurally the alternation of feasting with battling chapters begins with 'An Unexpected Party', followed by the more unpleasant interruption of the trolls' 'party' in 'Roast Mutton'. In Chapter Three 'The Short Rest' at Elrond's Last Homely House enables them to battle with goblins, Gollum, and wargs in the next three chapters until they rest at Beorn's 'Queer Lodging' in Chapter Seven. Battles with flies and spiders, wood-elves and raft-elves leave them grateful for the 'Warm Welcome' by the feasting men of Dale in Chapter Ten. Subsequent battles with the dragon, the dwarves, and then of the Five Armies weary them until the last two chapters where they return to Beorn's and Elrond's houses in 'The Return Journey' and to Bilbo's Bag End in 'The Last Stage'.

Symbolically the conflict between the hero and adversary is internalised within the split self of the protagonist. Bilbo for example is both Baggins and Took: he 'looked and behaved exactly like a second edition of his solid and comfortable father', a Baggins, but he had 'got something a bit *queer* in his makeup from the Took side, something that only waited for a chance to come out' (p. 17, my italics). The chance is provided by the visiting dwarves, who invite him to accompany them on their adventure as a professional burglar. The Tookish imagination in him, which is inherited from renegade hobbits who have themselves experienced adventures sporadically (p. 16), is swept away by the sound of Thorin's harp 'into dark lands under strange moons' (p. 26) so that he begins to yearn for the adventures he has earlier in the evening spurned (p. 18). His dormant imagination, expressed previously only through a love of neat smoke rings, flowers, and poetry (pp. 26, 19), awakens completely:

> As they sang the hobbit felt the love of beautiful things made by hands and by cunning and by magic moving through him, a fierce and jealous love, the desire of the hearts of dwarves. Then something Tookish woke up inside him, and he wished to go and see the great mountains, and hear the pinetrees and the waterfalls, and explore the caves, and wear a sword instead of a walking-stick. (p. 28)

This adventuresome imaginative self fully dominates Bilbo by the novel's end, for when he returns to the Shire 'He was in fact held by all the hobbits of the neighbourhood to be "queer" ' (p. 285). But the conflict between the Tookish side and the Baggins side begins much earlier. When he is accused of looking more like a grocer than a burglar by Gloin the dwarf on this same night, he realises: 'The Took side had won. He suddenly felt he would go without bed and breakfast to be thought fierce' (p. 30). It is indeed the grocer side of him he has defeated: the solid comfortable side appropriately named 'Baggins' as if in description of 'The Bag', both a pouch for storage of money or food and of course the stomach, which Bilbo will later call an 'empty sack' (p. 103). Even his house is called 'Bag End'. It is almost as if the Baggins side represents the temptations of the body as the Took side represents the desire for fulfilment of the soul. This desire is expressed through the image of the burglar which the Took side of Bilbo is asked to become.

Because burglars usually take things unlawfully from others, it is at first difficult to see how burglary will fulfil the spiritual or Took side of Bilbo. Yet it is more than a pun ('take'/'Took') for Bilbo: to steal requires physical dexterity and courage, some cunning and forethought, and in this particular case a love of his fellow creature. For Bilbo as burglar will merely retrieve for the dwarves that treasure which has been previously stolen from them by Smaug. Thus the dying Thorin will describe Bilbo as possessing 'Some courage and some wisdom, blended in measure' (p. 273). The quality the dwarf-king admires is temperance, that Augustinian moderation that almost seems Virtue itself. Indeed, when Bilbo renounces the arkenstone he has stolen, he resembles the greatest burglar, the *rex justus* Christ who gave up that humanity he had appropriated in order to redeem mankind.

Although Christ never actually appears in *The Hobbit*, still a type of Christ is provided in the figure of Gandalf. In *The Lord of the Rings* Gandalf dies as the 'Grey' and is reborn as the 'White' to suggest through colour imagery a parallel with Christ's own death and Resurrection. In *The Hobbit* he acts as a guide and teacher for Bilbo. Leading them through Rivendell and over the Misty Mountains up to Mirkwood, he protects them all from danger by supernatural means, mainly fire and magic wand, and encourages Bilbo by sparking his enthusiasm for the adventure with a few tales. Like any good parent, though, he realises he must depart (in

Chapter Seven) in order for Bilbo to develop his own physical, intellectual, and spiritual qualities as a burglar. When Bilbo achieves these, Gandalf returns as a *deus ex machina* (in Chapter Seventeen) to congratulate his pupil and to aid in the great Battle of the Five Armies.

Bilbo learns his trade as a burglar by defeating various monsters who collectively represent *amor sui*, love of self, but individually 'bodily' temptation and 'spiritual' temptation, as we have previously seen. In the process his physical bumbling at the beginning changes to real dexterity, then skill, and is finally aided by the courage of the newly-confident Bilbo. The way he defeats these adversaries in almost every case involves a type of burglary, as if in practice for the final and most crucial theft of the arkenstone. This first phase begins in the troll episode of the second chapter and concludes with his maturation as a brave burgling warrior in Chapter Eight, 'Flies and Spiders'.

He fails as a burglar in the troll episode because of poor timing and clumsiness. '"Silly time to go practising pinching and pocket-picking", said Bombur, "when what we wanted was fire and food"' (p. 52). He was asked by the dwarves to investigate the source of the light shining among the trees, not to put on the magic ring and pick the trolls' pockets. Still, he does 'steal' by accident the key to the troll cave. This shelter will afford them food and treasure (scabbards, hilts, sheaths) which they will 'steal' as they will later steal the cup and arkenstone from the dragon. In the second (Gollum) episode Bilbo is slightly more successful. He 'steals' Gollum's ring, again by accident, and he withstands Gollum's efforts as a mental burglar to discover 'What have I got in my pocket' (the ring, of course, p. 85). This theft is important because it provides him with the means to perform the burglary of the dragon's hoard – the invisibility caused by the ring. In addition it heightens his confidence in his new vocation. This allows him to demonstrate real heroism and leadership as a 'burglar' in Chapter Eight, 'Flies and Spiders'. He first shows purely physical skills: his keen sight spots a hidden boat that will let them cross the magic water; he prevents the other dwarves from falling in the water by snatching the rope they have been pulling; he climbs a tree to determine their location, thereby displaying his farsightedness and his light feet. But then he manifests more abstract qualities like courage. Asked to investigate a fire in the forest, he eventually saves his friends not from the elves whose festivities they have spotted but from the giant spiders who capture the dwarves while he sleeps under the elven spell. The first battle changes him: 'Somehow the killing of the giant spider, all alone by himself in the dark without the help of the wizard or the dwarves or of anyone else, made a great difference to Mr. Baggins. He felt a different person, and *much fiercer and bolder in spite of an empty stomach'* (p. 154, my italics). With this new boldness he 'steals' the captured dwarves, untying them after using his voice to lure the spiders away. He has learned from Gandalf's ventriloquism in the troll episode. He also kills six of the spiders with his sword Sting while rescuing Bombur, its new name a projection of the spider-like quality he now possesses after defeating the giant spider.

In Chapters Nine to Thirteen, Bilbo's burglaries depend more on his intellectual efforts than on his physical ones. After he becomes invisible to enter the Elvenking's castle where the dwarves are imprisoned, he devises the ruse of shutting them in wine barrels to allow his 'booty' to escape in the underground stream. Later, in Chapter Eleven, 'On the Doorstep', he can be a burglar only after he figures out a way of breaking into the tunnel leading to the dragon's lair. Much thinking and sitting take place before the thrush knocks at the grey stone, reminding Bilbo of the rune letters on the map which explain the setting sun on Durin's Day that will illuminate the keyhole into the rocky door. Finally, he uses both his imagination and his wit to trick the dragon into revealing its only vulnerable spot. After he steals the cup from the hoard he realises: 'Now he had become the real leader in their adventure. He had begun to have ideas and plans of his own' (p. 211). Part of these ideas involves posturing as a wise riddling poet to the dragon, for 'No dragon can resist the fascination of riddling talk and of wasting time trying to understand it' (p. 213). Further, Bilbo's flattery diverts the dragon so that he even shows off his magnificent diamond-studded waistcoat with its bare patch when Bilbo wonders whether dragons are softer underneath.

Now both courageous and wise, the hobbit becomes a burglar in the third and spiritual sense when he battles against that proud and avaricious monster inside himself. The dragon tempts him as his serpent forefather has tempted Adam in Eden: he intimates that the dwarves will never pay him a 'fair share'. Bilbo succumbs, stealing the precious arkenstone to ensure that he is paid for his work. 'Now I am a burglar indeed!' he cries (p. 226). Only in Chapter Sixteen, 'A Thief in the Night', does he forget about himself in his concern for others – the elves, men, and dwarves who may die from the approaching winter, starvation, or battle. He then relinquishes the arkenstone he has stolen from the dwarves to their enemies the elves and men, so that they may bargain with Thorin and end the dispute. This highly moral act redeems him: 'I may be a burglar – . . . but I am an honest one' (p. 257). He acts like the *Pastor bonus* St Augustine describes as the true king. Indeed, he now renounces all he has previously demanded in payment, taking away only two small chests of treasure and even making reparation to the Elvenking whose dwarf-prisoners he has stolen and whose bread he has eaten: 'some little return should be made for your, er, hospitality. I mean even a burglar has his feelings. I have drunk much of your wine and eaten much of your bread' (p. 277).

In giving to his 'host', Bilbo proves himself more than a guest, and the opposite of the burglar. In fact he becomes a host as well as an artist when he returns to the Shire, each role an expression of one of two sides, Baggins and Took. As the Baggins-grocer has demanded good financial terms for his work and his food in the very first chapter, so the new Baggins-host offers freely his tobacco and fire, physical commodities, to his friends. And as the Took-burglar has taken what is not his but also given it to someone else who needed it, so the new Took-artist offers freely what is never his to keep (experience and talent as expressed in poems and memoirs) to his future readers. The artist as hero is ultimately typified in Bard the Bowman, who saves Esgaroth by bravely killing the dragon but who continues to subordinate himself to the Master of Dale (p. 240). So Bilbo unifies his selves.

When Gandalf declares at the end that Bilbo has succeeded not because of personal luck but because of the general scheme of things – 'You are only quite a little fellow in a wide world after all' – Bilbo exclaims 'Thank goodness!' (pp. 286–7). In this last line of the novel Bilbo thanks the goodness of God as a universal and providential force for his selflessness, his littleness. He is indeed a 'child of the kindly West' living that life of the spirit characteristic of the Augustinian New Man or *novus homo*. He has progressed from the chronological maturity of a fifty-year old 'grown-up' (p. 17) to the state of wonder and joy common to the child – and the Christian. The cranky 'adult' Bilbo at the beginning snaps at Gandalf for interrupting his tea-party and chastises his 'child' Thorin once he emerges from his closed barrel: '"Well, are you alive or are you dead?'' Bilbo asked quite crossly. . . . ''If you want food and if you want to go on with this silly adventure – it's yours after all and not mine – you had better slap your arms and rub your legs''' (pp. 186–7). At the end this adult is transformed into the joyful, laughing, childlike Bilbo who welcomes his visitors Gandalf and Balin with a round of tobacco. As a child or childlike hobbit he must resemble those comprising the audience of *The Hobbit* – literal children, if the narrator's patronising remarks are any indication.

III The Narrator: the Critic under the Mask of the Children's Storyteller

The narrative intrusions – direct addresses to children, use of the first person singular, foreshadowing of later events, joking tone, plot clarifications, and sound effects intended for entertaining children[13] – have annoyed readers and critics. Yet they all constitute devices to create a narrative *persona* that functions as a character himself. Primarily he personifies the critic of the *Beowulf* lecture, or the adult or fairy-story teller (i.e., Andrew Lang) in the fairy-story lecture. He assumes that fairy-stories attract only children and probably function best as a bedtime narcotic to quiet restless boys and girls. As a tale teller he contrasts sharply with the wonderful Gandalf ('Tales and adventures sprouted up all over the place wherever he went, in the most extraordinary fashion', p. 17) and with the artist Tolkien, who is analogous to Chaucer the poet creating the character of Chaucer the pilgrim to introduce the Canterbury pilgrims – themselves tale tellers.

As a narrator he patronises his audience. He reminds them of details they may have forgotten, as when Bilbo crosses 'the ford beneath the steep bank, which you may remember' (p. 282) – but probably have forgotten, as it was crossed two hundred and fifty pages back. Like a literary critic he helps them understand the characters by delving beneath the surface: 'you will notice already that Mr. Baggins was not quite so prosy as he liked to believe, also that he was very fond of flowers' (p. 46). He adopts a falsely jovial tone, as when Bilbo has difficulty guessing Gollum's riddle: 'I imagine you know the answer, of course, or can guess it as easy as winking, since you are sitting comfortably at home and have not the danger of being eaten to disturb your thinking' (p. 83).

As a character he prides himself on his superior wisdom and

status as an adult. He is too busy to tell them even one or two songs or tales the dwarves heard at Elrond's house (p. 61). He belittles the silliness of legends like the one announcing a Took hobbit marriage to a fairy wife (p. 16). He expects the characters to emulate his adult wisdom and social decorum. Thus he applauds Bilbo's intelligent handling of Smaug by speaking riddles, but he criticises his growing reputation for queerness that results from visits to elves and poetry-writing (p. 285). A conformist socially, he especially dislikes signs of immaturity: when the dwarves ring the doorbell energetically he compares the action pejoratively to the mischievous pulling-off of the handle by a 'naughty hobbit-boy' (p. 22). He automatically assumes that his audience is the same size and shape as he, rather than four feet tall and light-footed like hobbits. He describes the hobbits, for example, as a 'little people, about half our height' who 'disappear quietly and quickly when large stupid folk like you and me come blundering along, making a noise like elephants which they can hear a mile off' (p. 16). To be smaller than he is to be abnormal: 'You must remember it [Gollum's tunnel] was not quite so tight for him [Bilbo] as it would have been for me or for you. Hobbits are not quite like ordinary people' (p. 77).

As a tale teller the narrator behaves more like a critic when he laughs at or disapproves of his characters, expressing neither pity nor terror at their plights which he relives vicariously. First he criticises Bilbo's unprofessional burgling in the troll episode:

> Either he should have gone back quietly and warned his friends that there were three fair-sized trolls at hand in a nasty mood, quite likely to try toasted dwarf, or even pony, for a change, or else he should have done a bit of good quick burgling. A really first-class and legendary burglar would at this point have picked the trolls' pockets – it is nearly always worthwhile, if you can manage it –, pinched the very mutton off the spits, purloined the beer, and walked off without their noticing him. (pp. 46–7)

In this critical attack and avaricious advice he resembles the dwarves who initially disbelieve in Bilbo's capabilities as a burglar, unlike Gandalf who trusts him implicitly from the beginning. When Bilbo does not see the edge of the forest as he peers from a tall tree just before they are captured by spiders, the narrator accuses him of lacking sense (p. 148). And when the dwarves worry about finding the entry to the Lonely Mountain, become depressed and demoralised, and only Bilbo has more spirit than they have, the narrator finds this 'strange'. He even underestimates the dwarves by labelling them as 'decent enough people . . . if you don't expect too much' (p. 204). For this reason he is not prepared for Thorin's charitable retraction at the moment of his death.

Perhaps most terribly, the narrator lacks compassion for and understanding of others. He reveals his cruelty when he confides that 'You would have laughed (from a safe distance), if you had seen dwarves sitting up in the trees with their beards dangling down' (p. 104). For the narrator the dwarves ready to be eaten chiefly provide amusement, not objects of sympathy. He also imagines that the audience laughs at Bilbo when the hero forgets there is no one to place the lid on *his* barrel so that he too can escape the wood-elves: 'Most likely you saw it [the weak spot in Bilbo's plan] some time ago and have been laughing at him' (p. 177). His lack of compassion renders him cruel and mean.

Loving only himself, in this pride and lack of charity the narrator becomes a monster like the dragon Smaug and the critic, who desires to be godlike in his acquisition of knowledge. This last King under the Mountain, or under the mask of the storyteller, seems to triumph undefeated by any hobbit hero. Yet Bilbo does have the last word, when Gandalf reminds him that he is 'only quite a little fellow in a wide world' (pp. 286–7) and Bilbo thanks goodness for this, at the very end. Perhaps the reader now notices the difference between the unobtrusive hobbit and the usually obtrusive narrator. Or perhaps the wordy and pompous narrator himself has learned something from this mere 'children's story'. So quiet now, maybe he is mute with wonder at the humiliating possibility that the small, childlike, queer Bilbo is 'right', after all.

3 The Christian King: Tolkien's Fairy-Stories

In the nineteenth century, fairy-tales were regarded as fantastic and trashy, and found little support from moralists and educationalists concerned with informing young minds: 'it would be absurd in such tales to introduce Christian principles as motives of action'.[1] In the twentieth century, in part due to the efforts of the Victorian compiler of fairy-tales Andrew Lang, fairy-stories have become for many parents and educators acceptable entertainment for children but have received little support from critics concerned with analysing great literature, if only because they are intended for children and not adults. Tolkien attempted to change this modern view by providing a literary aesthetic linking the fairy-story to Christian morality in his 1938 Andrew Lang Lecture, 'On Fairy-Stories', and by implementing that literary aesthetic in his own two fairy-stories, 'Leaf by Niggle' (written 1937–8, published 1945), and 'Smith of Wootton Major' (published 1967 but written years earlier[2]).

Considered by scholars not 'strictly a work of Faërie', these two stories have been criticised because they include 'a framing device set in the Primary World' and also 'a closely worked allegory'. 'True fantasy, according to Tolkien's own rule, takes place *inside* Faërie; there is no going to and from. . . . In both works Tolkien is presenting a message not a work of Faërie; true fantasy is nought but pure narrative, potent enough in the telling only and requiring no overlay of "meaning". Tolkien uses other devices to have his say *about* Faërie, and it seems that allegory is for him a favorite.'[3]

However, the message conveyed by these two supposed non-fairy stories has been subject to critical dispute. 'Leaf by Niggle' has been viewed as a fictionalised version of 'On Fairy-Stories',[4] but also as 'deeply Christian' – unlike 'Smith of Wootton Major' which is not 'overtly religious'.[5] In contrast, the latter has been perceived as autobiographical – reflecting the value of his art to Tolkien.[6]

Yet *both* of the stories outline in fiction the literary and moral aesthetic described in 'On Fairy-Stories'; *both* rely upon either an implicitly or explicitly Christian allegory that conjoins the primary to the secondary world. As we shall see, the secondary world of Faërie resembles the other world of Heaven, literally or figuratively, just as the primary world is our real world – that 'underworld' described by medieval writers as Hell. The primary world-frame remains necessary because both stories trace the transportation of the individual from this world to the other world. Such a need to contrast the two worlds in the fairy-story originated in Tolkien's early childhood: 'Quite by accident, I have a very vivid child's view, which was the result of being taken away from one country and put in another hemisphere – the place where I belonged but which was totally novel and strange. After the barren, arid heat a Christmas tree'.[7] The 'barren, arid heat' of Africa in December, Tolkien's early 'primary' world, resembles the dazzlingly fiery inferno of the medieval underworld in contrast to the joyous, cool 'other world' of England; the mention of the Christmas tree in this paradise also hints at Eden's Tree of Life, and the cross signifying Christ's salvation of mankind, to underscore the religious symbolism. His traumatic journey from one world to another so impressed the three-year-old Tolkien that the contrast informed his literary aesthetic long after he had matured, and he continued to use the tree as a major symbol of life as opposed to death, aridity, barrenness, throughout his literary career.

This new 'genre' of Tolkien differs from his previous accomplishments – his very scholarly editions, prefaces to editions, his lecture on *Beowulf* and other medieval articles – as well as from *The Hobbit*, a children's story more 'scholarly' and academic than these stories in that it incorporates Germanic heroic ideas included in the *Beowulf* lecture in addition to Christian notions of temptation and sin delineated in the *Ancrene Wisse* (the 'Guide of Anchoresses' discussed by Tolkien in a 1929 article and in 1962 edited critically for the Early English Text Society). Still, both *Beowulf* and Tolkien's

Beowulf lecture continued to influence this newly-shaped literary aesthetic despite the marked departure from past accomplishments, as the discussion of the lecture, 'On Fairy-Stories', and the two fairy-stories implementing the ideas contained in that lecture will show.

I 'On Fairy-Stories': Christ as Elf-King

'Beowulf: The Monsters and the Critics', Tolkien's Sir Israel Gollancz Lecture of 1936, defined the poem's central concern as this (primary) world – specifically, the forces of chaos and death on the Germanic level, and of sin and spiritual death on the Christian level – epitomised in the two monsters, Grendel and the Dragon, as Beowulf's chief adversaries, descended from Cain and Satan. respectively.[8] In contrast, 'On Fairy-Stories', in 1938, defines the fairy-tale's central concern as Faërie – a secondary world or Perilous Realm whose magic (unlike the sorrow, chaos, and unreason of Beowulf's primary world) satisfies the deepest human desires. Such desires include, first, the exploration of time and space, second, communication with other beings, and third, but most important of all,

> the oldest and deepest desire, the Great Escape: the Escape from Death. Fairy-stories provide many examples and modes of this – which might be called the genuine escapist, or I would say *fugitive* spirit. . . . Fairy-stories are made by men not by fairies. The Human-stories of the elves are doubtless full of the Escape from Deathlessness.[9]

In addition to the satisfaction of these desires, the fairy-story also supplies the Recovery of clear-sightedness, and Consolation, or Joy. *Beowulf*, then, belongs to a genre the antithesis of the fairy-story. Because it ends with the hero's death, the sorrow of his tragedy overwhelms the mood: the work imitates the dyscatastrophic tragedy discussed in 'On Fairy-Stories' and has been termed an elegy by Tolkien in the *Beowulf* lecture. But if the elegiac *Beowulf* ends with the triumph of chaos and death over man, then the fantastic fairy-story ends with the triumph of man over death and the escape into the other world. The agent of such triumph over death in fantasy is the supernatural guide, analogous in role to the death-allied monster of the elegy or tragedy. For Tolkien this guide is usually an elf or fairy.

The elf (or fairy – the terms are used equivocally in modern times, according to 'On Fairy-Stories', p. 9) is listed as an incubus or succubus, a demon, or a malignant being in the *OED*, in whose compilation Tolkien assisted. Like the *Beowulf* monsters, the elf can threaten man's spiritual well-being. In 'On Fairy-Stories' the elves and fairies represent tempters: 'part of the magic that they wield for the good or evil of man is power to play on the desires of his body and his heart' (p. 8). Yet elsewhere in 'On Fairy-Stories' and in Tolkien's own tales, the elves appear as guides of goodwill toward others, a nobler and wiser species than any other. Tolkien fondly cites Spenser's use of 'Elfe' to characterise the worthy and good knights of Faërie in *The Faerie Queene*: 'It [the name] belonged to such knights as Sir Guyon rather than to Pigwiggen armed with a hornet's sting' (p. 9). Like Sir Guyon in his bravery and virtue, the Red Cross Knight in the first book of *The Faerie Queene* battles with the Dragon in an allegorical three-day encounter complete with a Well and Tree of Life, after which he releases the King and Queen of Eden (Adam and Eve). This *Elfe* repeats the redemptive efforts of Christ as the second Adam.

The tie between the Elf-Prince and Christ is a strong one for Tolkien, who had read in the *Ancrene Wisse* that Jesus in His love for our soul functions as a king and noble knight in love with a lady: He 'came to give proof of His love, and showed by knightly deeds that He was worthy of love, as knights at one time were accustomed to do. He entered the tournament, and like a brave knight had His shield pierced through and through for love of His lady. His shield, concealing His Godhead, was His dear body, which was extended upon the cross'.[10]

For this reason the story of Christ in the Gospels is the penultimate fairy-story and the greatest fantasy of all time.

> The Gospels contain a fairy-story, or a story of a larger kind which embraces all the essence of fairy-stories . . . and among the marvels is the greatest and most complete conceivable eucatastrophe. . . . The Birth of Christ is the eucatastrophe of Man's history. The Resurrection is the eucatastrophe of the story of the Incarnation. ('On Fairy-Stories', pp. 71–2)

Reading about the 'character' Christ in this fairy-story of the

Gospels allows man to experience escape from the sorrow of this world and recovery and joy in the hope of another world – *the* Other World. All secondary worlds, all realms of Faërie in such fairy-stories ultimately are modelled upon Heaven. Entering Paradise remains the deepest fantasy of man because it constitutes the most important escape from death and from the stranglehold of this world on his life.

The difference between God's 'fairy-story' of the Gospels and fallen man's fairy-stories is that in the Gospels the primary world converges with the secondary world and creation becomes sub-creation: 'Art has been verified. God is the Lord, of angels, and of men – and of elves. Legend and History have met and fused' (p. 72). For once the happy ending has actually occurred in the normally tragic primary world; death has indeed died, in John Donne's words. But fallen man stains his own creation with the sin that darkens his glimpse of reality so that his view of the happy ending may be limited and even false. Just as the *Beowulf* poem displays two distinct levels, the Germanic and the Christian, because its author found himself caught in transition between two different ages, so the fairy-story similarly caught between two worlds possesses both a fallen and a redeemed (or perfect) form. For Tolkien 'All tales may come true; and yet, at the last, redeemed, they may be as like and as unlike the forms that we give them as Man, finally redeemed, will be like and unlike the fallen that we know' (p. 73). If man's fantasies which construct an imaginary secondary world could be 'redeemed' or realised they might indeed come true.

The fairy-story as a projection of man's hopes, desires, and fantasies embodies the ideals of the man behind the sub-creator. Similarly the fairy-story of the Gospels about the Word of God is itself the Word of God and thus represents God Himself. Christ's 'fairy-story' traces the happy turn of his life as man's fairy-stories trace the imagined happy turns of his life through *aventures* in perilous realms. For such reasons these tales must often become autobiographical, although only in the Bible is the 'autobiography' true: 'For the Art of it has the supremely convincing tone of Primary Art, that is, of Creation' (p. 72). If the stories often take the form of eucatastrophic legends not realisable in this world, then their sub-creation imitates in more humble form that of the Gospels: 'The Evangelium has not abrogated legends; it has hallowed them, especially the "happy ending" ' (p. 73). What this means is that the Christian who experiences joy and consolation after reading the fairy-story of the Gospels hopes for a similar happy ending to his life: 'The Christian has still to work, with mind as well as body, to suffer, hope, and die; but he may now perceive that all his bents and faculties have a purpose, which can be redeemed' (p. 73). When as sub-creator he projects this hope into the fantasy, his fairy-stories assume a religious and also a very personal cast.

Thus as a genre the fairy-story presents a 'sudden glimpse of the underlying reality or truth' (p. 71). This reality is perceived by man's heart or imagination rather than his head; Tolkien reveals an Augustinian bias toward faith and revelation, 'the eye of the heart', instead of the Aristotelian's 'eye of reason'.[11] He finds that the fantasy offers 'not only a "consolation" for the sorrow of this world' (like the consolation of Philosophy to Boethius for the sorrow produced by a world in which nothing lasts and in which all seems to be subject to Fortune's whims) but also a 'satisfaction, and an answer to that question, "Is it true?" ' (p. 71). Tolkien suggests that fantasy will be true for the reader if the secondary world it describes has been fashioned well and truly to inspire *belief*.

However, his prose non-fiction essay on fairy-stories is itself structured like the *Consolation of Philosophy* through the use of questions and answers, a technique that at first glance seems to appeal more to man's reason than to imagination and belief. The essay answers three questions: in the first section, 'What are fairy-stories?', in the second, 'What is their origin?', and in the following four, 'What is the use of them?' Yet in the first sentences of his essay he cautions potential explorers of fairy-stories (he himself is a 'wandering explorer' and not a 'professional') *not* to 'ask too many questions, lest the gates should be shut and the keys be lost' (p. 3). The truth of which he speaks here springs from magic and cannot be captured by the scientist's question-and-answer techniques. The scientist's tendency to reduce the whole by analysing it into parts in this manner clashes with the artist's tendency to see the whole and with the reader's tendency to ask of the whole story, is it real? His studies of fairy-story elements 'are . . . scientific (at least in intent); they are the pursuit of folklorists or anthropologists: that is of people using the stories not as they were meant to be used, but as a quarry from which to dig evidence, or information, about matters in which they are interested' (p. 18).

What Tolkien has written in this essay is certainly not a fairy-story or a fantasy but its opposite. As Literature (especially fantasy) sub-creates a secondary world with its characteristic eucatastrophe, so Drama mirrors the primary world with its characteristic dyscatastrophe. This essay, dramatic non-fiction portraying those clashes between Tolkien as artist-hero or lover of fairy-stories and the critic-as-monster, reflects the battling and sorrow common to the real world. In the introduction he sides with the lover of fairy-stories against the question-asking professional scientist. In Section One he argues with an invisible critic who believes fairy-stories concern diminutive creatures conceived by limited imaginations. In Section Two, 'Origins', he traces the convergence of history and myth in the Soup of tales, frustrating the scientist and compiler interested in identifying the ingredients of the Soup. In Section Three, 'Children', he opposes Lang and similar educationalists and parents who intend the fairy-story for the child and not the adult, the latter of whom in many cases desires more than the child to escape from this world and to believe in another: 'Let us not divide the human race into Eloi and Morlocks: pretty children – "elves" as the eighteenth century often idiotically called them – with their fairy tales (carefully pruned), and dark Morlocks tending their machines' (p. 45). In Section Four, 'Fantasy', he analyses the differences between Literature and Drama, the latter the especial province of the critic. In Section Five, 'Recovery, Escape, Consolation', he contrasts the secondary world with the primary, and the effects of both on man. Only in Section Six, 'Epilogue', does a 'eucatastrophe' occur, a happy ending which reveals that a fairy-story (the Gospels) *is* true, and provides the model for all other fairy-stories. But only the Christian will believe in Tolkien's eucatastrophe because such belief is a matter of faith and not of reason. And perhaps only the Christian will perceive the genre of this non-fiction 'fairy-story' as eucatastrophic, with the monstrous clashes between the critic and the artist in this work triumphantly resolved.

The accompanying fairy-story, 'Leaf by Niggle', with which the essay appeared in 1964–5 in *Tree and Leaf*, and 'Smith of Wootton Major' more clearly embody the aesthetic principles and genre discussed in 'On Fairy-Stories'. They also more clearly illustrate, as fictional autobiography, those central Christian truths and joys projected by Tolkien the sub-creator into his fantasy. Indeed, these two incarnate the 'description of two moments in a great life, rising and setting; an elaboration of the ancient and intensely moving contrast between youth and age, first achievement and final death', which Tolkien clarified as the structure of *Beowulf* in his lecture (p. 81). 'Leaf by Niggle' was written first in 1938–9 and projects the fears of the 'rising' artist-as-hero (Tolkien had just finished *The Hobbit*, and had recently started 'The New Hobbit') that worldly demands might frustrate the completion of his work before his death. Second, 'Smith of Wootton Major', which was published in 1967 although written years earlier, as a 'setting moment' in the career of an artist who had finally finished the mammoth epic of *The Lord of the Rings* projects his final, peaceful acceptance, and even his joy, at the relinquishing of his artistic gift. Because both fairy-stories end in eucatastrophic turns, neither can be considered a work of 'setting', of death, even though the second work describes the end of the artist's career and the first describes the younger artist's imagined 'death'. Both attempt to portray the Great Escape *from* death.

If *The Hobbit*, as we have suggested, constitutes Tolkien's attempt to rewrite *Beowulf* as a fairy-story fantasy with a eucatastrophic ending rather than an heroic elegy,[12] then 'Leaf by Niggle' and 'Smith of Wootton Major' provide the next step in the fictional metamorphosis of his literary aesthetic. Using the Andrew Lang essay as a springboard, Tolkien rewrites his own life as a fairy-story, moving backward from the true secondary world of the hobbits to the traumatic and awkward convergence of primary and secondary worlds in his own life. Not his aspirations as a medieval scholar, philologist, and teacher but his hopes and fears as a man, an artist, and a Christian surface in these two stories. It is appropriate that the synthesising and harmonising art of Tolkien, which sought always to wed his diverse sides, depicted in these stories a sub-creation in which angels and elves, Christ and Fairy-Kings, meet. True, the *Beowulf* monsters reappear – but depicted as *human* characters, flawed, suffering from various sins and subordinated to the Christian saviour-heroes. The monster in 'Leaf' is Parish and also Tompkins, the critical neighbour and councillor, like the destructive critics Tolkien denigrates in his *Beowulf* lecture; the monster in 'Smith' is Nokes, the proud, critical Master Cook who reigns over the kitchen as evilly as the various 'kings under the mountain' in *The Hobbit*. But Tolkien's real interest in these joyous fairy-stories centres on the figure of the Elf, a Christlike figure and agent of good. The merciful Second Voice in

'Leaf' allows the artist Niggle to enter a consoling secondary world or an Other World; the Elf-King Alf in 'Smith' similarly provides consolation to the artist Smith who must give up his visits to the secondary world. Man caught between this and the Other World, divided between his Niggle and his Parish sides (in the medieval sense, between the angel and the beast), ultimately freely chooses the good, as does Smith when confronted with the choice by Alf – at least, in Tolkien's own autobiographical, heavily Christian and allegorical fairy-tales.

II 'Leaf by Niggle': the Second Voice and Niggle

That 'Leaf by Niggle' is the most heavily Christian and allegorical of any of Tolkien's fiction is clear; exactly how Christian, despite the vestigial Germanic concepts inherited from the *Beowulf* lecture/*Hobbit* phase of his career, has not been fully revealed. Along with 'Smith of Wootton Major' it forms a Christian parable that neatly exemplifies those basic concepts illustrated for example in the *Ancrene Wisse*. In this 'Guide for Anchoresses' or conduct book outlining the process of self-discipline for the Christian, eight major sections emerge which the translator (but not the medieval author in the manuscript Tolkien edited) has labelled appropriately 'Devotions', 'Custody of the Senses', 'Regulation of the Inward Feelings', 'Temptations', 'Confession', 'Penance', 'Love', and 'External Rules'. Earlier, Tolkien used some of these sections to guide Bilbo's transformation into a Christian-like artist-hero in *The Hobbit*, specifically the sections on 'Custody of the Senses', 'Regulation of the Inward Feelings', and, as the culmination of the disciplinary process, the withstanding of 'Temptations' both bodily and spiritual. Now in 'Leaf' he seems to use the next sections, 'Confession' and 'Penance', especially: as a 'rising moment' in Tolkien's literary autobiography the story dramatises the Catholic sacrament of Penance through the hard work justly warranted by Niggle's artistic inadequacies, followed only much later by the merciful Gentle Treatment he receives. In contrast in 'Smith' he seems to use the next-to-last section of the *Ancrene Wisse*, 'Love': as a 'setting moment' in Tolkien's life the story celebrates fully the power of Smith's love or *amor Dei* rewarded by the gift of grace.

The title of 'Leaf by Niggle' possesses two significations which unify the major themes of the tale. First, referring to the torn fragment of canvas adorned by the single leaf created by Niggle and discovered by Atkins the schoolmaster, who hangs it in the museum which along with the Leaf burns down later, it emblematises the effects of the primary world on all material things. Second, it refers to Niggle's original impulse to create a single, perfect leaf on canvas, but one which he accomplishes only in the secondary world he enters after leaving the Workhouse; as such it emblematises the changelessness and absolute perfection or the eternal Idea of all matter in a very Neo-Platonic other world – 'All the leaves he had ever laboured at were there, as he had imagined them rather than as he had made them.'[13]

Moreover, these associations typifying the two worlds are inexorably linked in Christian tradition through the symbol of the tree. Because our first parents ate of the fruit of the Tree of Knowledge of Good and Evil, they were expelled from paradise, forced to wander the wilderness in exile, and condemned like their descendants to suffer the effects of sin, or death and mutability. So it is ironic that Niggle captures in oils a single leaf – which is eventually destroyed by that mutability which resulted from their original sin. The cross, too, on which Christ, the second Adam, was crucified was frequently regarded as a 'tree' constructed from the same wood as the Tree of Life, the other tree appearing in Paradise, in order to anticipate the power of His love in overcoming the sin of Adam and redeeming all mankind. And in medieval representations of the Garden of Paradise a Tree of Life also appears.[14] Again ironically, just as the torn leaf connotes Niggle's failure as an artist to complete his life's work because of constant interruptions for menial reasons, so the ideal leaf parallels the gentle treatment offered to him as a reward for his charity, or success as a human being in helping his neighbour in this world even though his own ambitions as an artist are thwarted. Niggle is permitted to enter a paradise where his travails as an artist are not only perfectly conceived but perfectly implemented. The two worlds in which the torn and the ideal leaves have their beings are drawn from Neo-Platonic as well as Christian commonplaces.

Macrobius in the fourth century and his commentators in later centuries, especially the twelfth, conceived of our world as an 'abode of Dis', the lower regions of the universe, or the *infernum* (both the inferior and fallen regions, and the underworld, or Hell).[15] But there was a second underworld, equally fallen and inferior – the body in which the soul after journeying through the spheres of the supernal regions was incarcerated. Like the under-world it was regarded as tomb-like or prison-like because it forced the soul to endure the corruption of corporeality in this world. It is this prison-like underworld that dominates both 'Leaf by Niggle' and also Tolkien's conception of the primary world. In 'On Fairy-Stories', Tolkien vehemently condemns the twentieth-century world for its burgeoning technology and dehumanised values and promotes the idea of Escape by the return to the past or to another world: 'Why should a man be scorned if, finding himself in prison, he tries to get out and go home? Or if, when he cannot do so, he thinks and talks about other topics than jailers and prison-walls?' (p. 60). The prison metaphor picks up the Neo-Platonic and Macrobian associations of the under- (primary) world – a metaphor Tolkien also uses in 'Leaf by Niggle' to characterise the Purgatory-like Workhouse and, through the rigidity and stern-ness of the many jailer-like officials governing the primary world, the actual world in which Niggle must struggle as an artist.

The Neo-Platonists also conceived of an overworld – a superior Aplanon called 'paradisus' in Greek, 'ortus' in Latin, and 'Eden' in Hebrew – from which souls depart at birth and to which they return at death. In this world all exists as Idea to be translated by the World Soul into fallen and earthly living images destined for life on earth.[16] It is this superior Aplanon to which Niggle proceeds for 'Gentle Treatment' and where he locates the perfect leaf which his earthly artistry only imperfectly copied. The major Idea of Niggle which metamorphoses into image on earth is the Idea of the leaf: he *is* his art, or his self as an artist is one with his artistic ideas (just as 'Tolkien' refers both to the man and to his works). Only in the other world can Niggle 'be' himself ideally. Further, what he has accomplished on earth as an artist constitutes his reward in the other world: Tolkien reworks the Christian convention of Good Works into a fairy-story framework.

Tolkien has also reworked the Christian convention of the earthly conflict between soul and body into his fairy-story. Niggle and Parish personify the two sides of man that inevitably clash in this world because each is pulled in a different direction, although they eventually enjoy a harmonious 'collaboration' (resurrection) in the other world after the fantasy equivalent of 'death'. Etymologically their names reflect their natures as personifications of the complementary sides of the macrocosm and of the micro-cosm man. The verb 'niggle', apparently derived from Scandinavian, means (according to the *OED*) 'to work, or do anything, in a trifling, fiddling, or ineffective way; to trifle (*with* a thing); to spend work or time unnecessarily on petty details; to be over-elaborate in minor points'. The ineffective worker Niggle suggests the microcosmic counterpart of the parish, or Parish, which, again in the *OED*, refers not necessarily only to the charge of a bishop or presbyter but also to a county subdivision used for civic and local government, that geographical area dependent upon the work of its governing officials. If 'Parish' personifies the practical and economic needs of a geographical area, then 'Niggle' personifies the earthly failure to supply those needs, a failure overseen and condemned by various Inspectors of Houses and Gardens and various government officials who seem to make Parish's interests their business. In the other world, however, these two eventually harmonise their efforts in a change reflected through the names of the geographical areas they inhabit, construct, and control. Although Niggle first arrives at a place called 'Niggle', after he gardens and builds it becomes 'Niggle's Country', then, given the burgeoning of Parish's garden, 'Niggle's Parish'. The last name perfectly epitomises the harmony between the artist and the gardener, the sub-creator and sub-creation, which results in this paradise. Truly a whole and single world as well as a whole and single self emerges, rather than a primary world divided and warring and a self fragmented and divided as they have been on earth. More microcosmically the names illustrate these complementary sides of the self. 'Niggle' also means 'to trot about, keep moving *along*' in a fiddling or ineffective manner, which perfectly describes his activity as 'legs' or 'messenger' for the lame Parish and his bedridden, ill wife. Finally the names echo the complementary roles of the artist and the gardener used by Tolkien as metaphors for the soul and the body. Thus Niggle means 'to cheat, trick', plus, in its nominative form, someone who 'niggles', especially in artistic work: he resembles as a niggling or cheating artist the artist-as-burglar embodied in Bilbo of *The Hobbit*. The Parish who prunes real flowers, plants, and trees represents the opposite of the artist who draws or paints on canvas a single leaf.

On earth Niggle the kindhearted artist and Parish the critical gardener struggle for mastery like soul and body, one against the other. Niggle, lazy, kindhearted, imaginative and giving, portrays the Heart itself: 'He could not get rid of his kind heart. ''I wish I was more strong-minded,'' he sometimes said to himself, meaning that he wished other people's troubles did not make him feel uncomfortable' (p. 89). Faced with interruptions by visitors, friends, and Parish, he dare not say no (p. 90). In contrast Parish lacks warmth and imagination: he is practical, commonsensical, rational. Critical of Niggle's garden and what he sees as 'green and grey patches and black lines' in his paintings, he dismisses them as 'nonsensical' (p. 91). A gardener who tends to the raising of food rather than spirits and excessively concerned about house repairs and illnesses, Parish demands help from his neighbour the artist who cares primarily about 'work' only in the sense of art.

Parish also symbolises the Macrobian underworld as Niggle symbolises the overworld. As the name of a *place* 'Parish' symbolises the inferior, infernal regions of the earth; as the name of a *person* he symbolises the underworld of the inferior body into which the superior soul is plunged. In 'Leaf by Niggle' Tolkien recognises this by making the lower primary world in character like Parish, just as Niggle as a symbol of the soul in the individual and of the overworld or paradise resembles the Other World in *his* character, an idea underscored by the initial naming of the overworld 'Niggle'.

Parish criticises Niggle's efforts as an artist to the point where Niggle wishes that Parish would provide 'help with the weeds (and perhaps praise for the pictures)' (p. 91), instead of ignoring his painting and criticising his garden. Similarly, the human officials governing this world ignore spiritual or imaginative activities and criticise, through the enforcing of rigorous laws, infractions of their concern with material goods like the garden produce that serves to feed the body, if not the soul. Such stern laws so dominate all human life – 'The laws . . . were rather strict' (p. 90) – that when Niggle has to serve on a *jury* (law, once again) and thereby neglects his own garden his visitors warn him of a probable visit from an Inspector. Providing for the needs of the body such as food to satisfy hunger, a house to shelter, medicine to quell illness, *is* the usual activity of man; inactivity in this sense invites punishment. Individual freedom of choice is lacking because neighbour *must* help neighbour no matter what personal feeling dictates. When Parish's house is deemed unsatisfactory Niggle is blamed for not helping him roof it with his canvas: 'houses come first. That is the law' (p. 95). Like Parish, who regards painting as having no practical or economical use, the House Inspector looks at Niggle's painting workshop and sees only things: 'There is plenty of *material* here: canvas, wood, waterproof paint' (p. 95, my italics). Material good becomes an end in itself because of the nature of this world, imbued with sickness and death for the individual, storm and catastrophe for the larger world, the macrocosm. Parish goes lame, his wife catches a fever, and Niggle experiences chills and fever before dying: Niggle's garden needs tending, Parish's house needs repairs, and the storm both damages the house and causes Niggle to become ill. The house constantly requires repair and the Museum is lost through fire; the body, similarly, succumbs to illness, dies, and is forgotten after death. Things do not last. Even more Parish-like than the Inspectors who check for violations of the law are the human 'judges' who comment after his death on Niggle's worth as a man, for they carry Parish's perceptions and criticisms to an extreme. Condemning Niggle's art ('private day-dreaming'), the literalistic and materialistic Councillor Tompkins sees in Niggle's painting only the 'digestive and genital organs of plants'; he totally misunderstands the spiritual value of the painting and its restorative effects. Because his judgement is impaired and blinded, this human 'king' or 'councillor' wrongly condemns Niggle as a 'footler' who should have been relegated either to 'washing dishes in a communal kitchen or something' or to being 'put away' before his time (p. 110). He is blinded in his judgement by his own selfish greed or his *cupiditas*: because he has always wanted, and eventually obtains, Niggle's house for his own, he must rationalise this action by dismissing the man as insignificant. Even though Atkins the schoolmaster sees great value in Niggle's painting – 'I can't get it out of my mind' (p. 111) – and goes so far as to rescue and then frame and hang the surviving leaf in the local museum, it is Tompkins' view that dominates the dialogue – just as mutability obliterates all trace of Niggle and his art from existence in this world as if he were indeed insignificant and inconsequential.

If Niggle while on earth does not measure up to the expectations of his neighbour Parish, the Inspectors, and Councillor Tompkins because he is not interested in gardens and houses, neither does he measure up to the expectations of the Workhouse Infirmary doctors and to a certain extent the members of the Court of Inquiry convened after he recuperates in the Infirmary, but for a very different reason. On earth he has been distracted by the requests of his neighbour and of his community from preparing for his 'Journey' (presumably after death), which incurs the wrath of the

Workhouse officials. Thus, like the somewhat distracted Christian who sins too often during life in this world, he must endure the rigours of this harsh, prison-like Purgatory. His status almost resembles that of the first and lowest class of the Elect described in the 'Penance' section of the *Ancrene Wisse*. These good pilgrims are 'sometimes pleased by what they see on their way, and they pause a little, while not quite stopping, and many things happen to them to hinder them, and this is the worse for them, for some arrive home late and some never at all' (p. 155). While Niggle is not pleased at all by Parish's interruptions of his work, still he is hindered in arriving 'home' and is punished accordingly for it, making his 'Escape' from the prison of this world very late and very badly. In a sense he makes it not at all – for this new world he inhabits resembles the worst of the old world.

Because he has prepared inadequately for his 'Journey', without packing any luggage or finishing his work, he is confined to the Workhouse Infirmary, given bitter medicine and unfriendly, strict ministrations by attendants and a severe doctor – 'It was more like being in a prison than in a hospital' (p. 97) – and denied any freedom of choice to work at his own leisure, or even any leisure. The emphasis on law here is similar to that in the real world but understood more abstractly: Niggle does not have to complete a specific task like preparing for a journey but to discipline himself or to subordinate desire and the self to law, duty, and reason. He must manage to keep 'Custody of the Senses' as demanded of the recluse in the *Ancrene Wisse* and become 'dead' to the world, feeling neither sorrow nor joy, as if he had risen to the status of the second class of the Elect (described in 'Penance'). He carpenters and paints houses 'all one plain colour' without feeling any joy: 'poor Niggle got no pleasure out of life. . . . But . . . he began to have a feeling of – well, satisfaction: bread rather than jam' (p. 98). Now self-disciplined, in contrast to his previous procrastination and inefficiency on earth, 'He had no "time of his own" (except alone in his bed-cell), and yet he was becoming master of his time' (p. 98). He suffers the hardship of plain digging instead of the luxury of plain carpentry and painting and this breaks him physically – 'his back seemed broken, his hands were raw' (p. 98) – but cures him spiritually. He worries about what he might have done better for Parish, he learns peace, rest, and satisfaction from doing work well and efficiently, and eventually he so forgets previous curses and gripes as to achieve a total serenity of mind

and love of Other. He comes ultimately to resemble members of
the third class of the Elect, those 'hung with consent on Jesus'
cross' (p. 154) who experience joy in suffering. What this suffering
involves in the *Ancrene Wisse* is climbing the ladder of Penance with
'Dishonour and hardship . . . the two sides of the ladder which go
straight up to heaven, and between these sides are fixed the rungs
of all the virtues by which men climb to the happiness of heaven'
(p. 157). Specifically, hardship occurs 'in the face of injustice when
one suffers the ignominy of being accounted worthless' (p. 157).
After Niggle endures the labour or physical hardship of the
Workhouse, he indeed suffers so: counted a 'silly little man. . . .
Worthless, in fact; no use to Society at all' (p. 110) by Councillor
Tompkins on earth, he is also regarded as 'only a little man. . . .
never meant to be anything very much' (p. 99) by the Second Voice
in the dark outside his Workhouse room. Yet he reveals perfect
humility when he voices his concern for his former neighbour
Parish before the Second Voice and when he feels shame over
being singled out for Gentle Treatment – 'To hear that he was
considered a case for Gentle Treatment overwhelmed him, and
made him blush in the dark. It was like being publicly praised,
when you and all the audience knew that the praise was not
deserved. Niggle hid his blushes in the rough blanket' (p. 101). But
this very humility has earned him 'Gentle Treatment'. Labour and
humility, 'in which all penance consists', allow these third members of the Elect to receive in the Other World the joy of honour for
dishonour or humility and delight and eternal rest for suffering or
hardship. Interestingly, Tolkien echoes this very Christian sentiment in 'On Fairy-Stories' when he indicates that 'fairy-stories are
not the only means of recovery, or prophylactic against loss.
Humility is enough' (p. 58). Niggle's 'education' as a 'Christian'
has involved passing through the three stages described in the
Ancrene Wisse dominated by the three classes of Elect who undergo
the rigours of Penance. His progress or lack of it at every level has
been evaluated by various judges, human and superhuman.

He is first judged inconsequential by a human judge (Tompkins)
because he ignores worldly concerns, and is then judged as a
partial failure in completing his own duties to himself (preparing
for the journey by finishing his artistic rather than his worldly
work – this is, after all, a *Work*house, where how one performs
one's job, whatever it may be, even painting, does count). But he is
finally judged in the more important Court of Inquiry as deserving

Gentle Treatment. A failure as a gardener and as an artist, he succeeds as *a good man* when judged by the Two Voices. It is partly as a result of the mercy of the Second Voice and not as a result of the justice of the First Voice that he is accorded Gentle Treatment – or grace.

The 'severe' First Voice of course represents the fantastic equivalent of God the Father, the First Person of the Trinity suggesting Old Testament wrath. Such Justice contrasts with the New Testament Mercy characteristic of the 'gentle' God the Son, the Second Person of the Trinity. The dialogue between the two in the Workhouse-world of Purgatory echoes the dialogue between their foils, Tompkins and Atkins, the practical politician and the wise, gentle schoolmaster, in the primary world – or even between Parish and Niggle, personifications of the two sides of each individual. The First Voice denigrates Niggle's various moral weaknesses, as the Second Voice, whose role it is to 'put the best interpretation on the facts' (p. 101), finds in contrast his moral strengths. When the Second Voice declares, 'His heart was in the right place', the First Voice counters with 'Yes, but it did not function properly. . . . And his head was not screwed on tight enough: he hardly ever thought at all' (p. 99). Even though the First Voice, in the best Old Testament fidelity to the letter, accuses him of neglecting 'too many things ordered by the law' (p. 100), the Second Voice's defence wins Gentle Treatment for him because he stresses his humility and service to his neighbour Parish. Niggle has portrayed beautiful leaves in paint but 'never thought that that made him important' and has served Parish by answering many appeals for which 'he never expected any Return' (p. 100). His greatest sacrifice occurred during the wet bicycle ride, when he realised that he was relinquishing his last chance to finish the picture and that Parish did not really need him that desperately. He sacrificed himself for his neighbour in the most Christlike fashion.

The mercy of the Second Voice permits Niggle to enter Niggle's Country for an eternity of rest and convalescence wherein he eventually enjoys the pleasure (and grace) of coming 'home' to his painting. Tolkien here illustrates the virtues of Faërie's secondary world in this 'world' called Niggle, the virtues of Escape, Recovery, and Consolation. Usually entry into a secondary world occurs for Tolkien through the reading of fairy-stories whose fantasy guarantees a sub-creation which offers these three virtues. In 'Leaf',

Niggle 'dies' and because of his Christian humility – a second means of entry into a secondary world – 'recovers' or is reborn and redeemed. His recovery follows the pattern outlined by Tolkien in his definition in 'On Fairy-Stories': 'Recovery (which includes return and renewal of health) is a re-gaining . . . of a clear view . . . "seeing things as we are (or were) meant to see them" – as things apart from ourselves' (p. 57). The first step is physical, the renewal of health, followed by the second, more figurative and spiritual step, recovery of true vision.

Thus, after Niggle in the Workhouse *Infirmary* heals with the help of the doctor's medicines, he is then offered Gentle Treatment (the term itself implies an illness) and he and Parish drink from a bottle of tonic that eases the tiredness experienced soon after their arrival. Most of all it is the place, 'Niggle', that restores them through its sub-creative gifts 'as a holiday, and a refreshment. It is splendid for convalescence. . . . It works wonders in some cases' (p. 112). The metaphor of sickness on earth (fever, lameness, chills) and of recovery of health in the secondary world is beautifully handled in the story.

Niggle's recovery and that of Parish includes as well the clearing of vision. When Niggle first enters his Country he *sees* immediately that some of the most beautiful leaves 'were seen to have been produced in collaboration with Mr. Parish'. This fact surprises him (p. 104) because he always considered that 'collaboration' as interruption. Now he realises that Parish remains very necessary to his work, for 'There are lots of things about earth, plants, and trees that he knows and I don't' (pp. 105–6). Similarly Parish sees his former neighbour clearly and finally understands and appreciates his artistry as restorative: 'Did *you* think of all this, Niggle? I never knew you were so clever' (p. 109).

Both as well escape from suffering the 'hunger, thirst, poverty, pain, sorrow, injustice' and death characteristic of the primary world ('On Fairy-Stories', pp. 65–6), to receive Consolation in the secondary world. The usually kindhearted Niggle in this world grumbled and complained to himself after Parish made his requests; even Parish was a critical, sour, grim-mouthed neighbour. Once Niggle reached the Workhouse he became 'quieter inside now' – less angry and more tolerant and gentle. Now in 'Niggle' both men alter their moods tremendously. They sing merrily while they plan and plant gardens; eventually, having arrived at the uppermost reaches of the Mountains, they fully reveal their joy when they learn of the 'happy catastrophe', the name of their country being Niggle's Parish. 'They both laughed. Laughed – the Mountains rang with it!' (p. 112). Recovery, Escape, Consolation – such fantastic virtues transform, even redeem and resurrect, Parish and Niggle as opposites and collaborators. The Gospels *are* a fairy-story, after all. And the artist as sub-creator, the 'practical' architect of the secondary world as is Niggle of Niggle's Country, desperately needs the lover of art or the reader of fairy-stories, who is liberated by the fantasy of fairy-stories to escape his real-life function and character, or his Parish-side, in order to complete him.

III 'Smith of Wootton Major': Alf the Elf-King and Smith

While less obviously Christian and allegorical than 'Leaf by Niggle', 'Smith of Wootton Major' still emphasises Christian themes and concepts. As a 'setting moment' describing what must have seemed like the end of Tolkien's career as a writer, 'Smith' provides the ultimate consolation for the good Christian – the reward of grace for humility and suffering. Unlike 'Leaf', in 'Smith' no punishment or stern, literalistic judging of the individual occurs. Here suffering is valuable because God may reward it – may 'turn towards it with His grace, and make the heart pure and clear-sighted, and this no one may achieve who is tainted with vices or with an earthly love of worldly things, for this taint affects the eyes of the heart so badly that it cannot recognise God or rejoice in the sight of him' (p. 170). This quotation from 'Love', the seventh section of the *Ancrene Wisse*, beautifully summarises the pure spiritual condition of the child Smith. Because free of vice and filled with charity he is 'graced' with the gift of the star, his passport into the other world of Faërie, but one which simultaneously endows him with a recovery of insight and perception because of his visits to the other world. And the love of Smith for his family and for his fellow man and ultimately for God stems from a pure heart: 'A pure heart, as St. Bernard says, effects two things: it makes you do all that you do either for the love of God alone, or for the good of others for His sake' (p. 170), an Augustinian pronouncement springing from the pages of the *Ancrene Wisse*.

Humility and love find expression in his behaviour both before the star is bestowed upon him and at the moment he must return the star. While children in Wootton Major seem in general more likely to appreciate the magnificent Master Cakes baked every twenty-four years, only a child graced with charity (St Augustine's true New Man) receives the gift of insight. Smith, who has given up the silver coin he found in his piece of cake to the luckless Nell who discovered nothing in hers, manifests that fine charity that enables him to qualify for the fairy star.[17] When the time comes for him to relinquish the star, note that Smith also gives it up because someone else needs it (pp. 41 and 44). His lifelong concern for others earns him the right to choose the new recipient of the star – Nokes of Townsend's Tim, the great-grandson of the Master Cook Nokes. Such a choice well illustrates his insight into human nature but also a markedly Christian attitude of beatitudinal meekness and love of those who are different – 'he's not an obvious choice', says Smith (p. 47). Even Tim himself portrays the same humility and selflessness: he requests only a very *small* piece of cake (p. 57) without demanding more than he can eat.

Such humility and love motivate Alf's behaviour as well: he endures quietly the chagrin of being Nokes' apprentice and receiving no recognition for his work. His love is manifested toward man: he gives up years in Faërie for the opportunity to be the insignificant Prentice in the primary world. Here he patiently waits for the opportunity, first, to slip the fairy star into Nokes' cake, then, years and years later, to slip it into his very own last Great Cake for Tim. Alf or Elf typifies the apprentice to the master whose humility leaves him always ready to learn and whose selflessness and love make him ready to serve others. That is, he signifies the eternal youth or *novus homo*, the youngness of the spirit rather than the oldness of pride and the senses. After living in Wootton Major a short time as an apprentice, 'He had grown a bit taller but still looked like a boy, and he had only served for three years' (p. 13). Ironically it is because of his youth that the townspeople do not regard him as an obvious choice to replace the old master and instead they choose Nokes. Generously lending his great skill to the proud and ambitious Nokes, he serves the community humbly and well for years. Even at the very end, long after Smith has aged, Alf remains youthful: he 'looked like the apprentice of long ago, though more masterly' (p. 40). (His queen also appears to be a 'young maiden' when first espied by Smith.)

But the opposites of humility and love – arrogance and selfishness, or *cupiditas* – are exemplified in Nokes. While the zeal of Faërie is directed toward the higher imaginative and moral pursuits of art and immortality, the zeal of the primary world – here Wootton Major – is directed toward material goods, specifically as symbolised by cooking. Appropriately, excessive interest in physical sustenance, the senses, literalness, leads to a spiritual oldness characterised by greed, pride, *cupiditas* in general. The *Ancrene Wisse* speaks of gluttony in terms of a cooking metaphor: 'The greedy glutton is the devil's manciple, but he is always about the cellar or the kitchen' (p. 96). Nokes insists on being if not performing as the Master Cook and similarly puts himself before others because he lacks both humility and charity. A literal old man by the end of the story, he remains interested in the mystery of food but misunderstands or totally ignores higher forms of sustenance. His clashes with Alf dramatise the Christian confrontation between Satan (or a Satan-figure) and the Second Person of the Trinity. Called eventually a 'vain old fraud, fat, idle and sly' by Alf, in his size and age he illustrates gluttony, materialism, and the oldness of literalism. At the beginning of the story he patronises the children at the Feast by giving them what he thinks they deserve: 'Fairies and sweets were two of the very notions he had about the tastes of children. Fairies he thought one grew out of; but of sweets he remained very fond' (p. 14). Like Andrew Lang and the narrator of *The Hobbit* he assumes that 'small' and 'young' signify 'inferior'. So Nokes similarly misunderstands the deceptive youthfulness of Alf: 'You'll grow up someday' (p. 16). To Nokes growing up involves the development of a materialism similar to his 'adult' values. Thus he regards the unusual and different fay star, the passport to Faërie, as 'funny', something intended to make the children laugh. He lacks imagination as well as the youthfulness characterising the life of the spirit. Puzzled by the seeming disappearance of that fay star, he projects a practical and materialistic interpretation of the mystery on to the facts: he imagines first that *Molly* got the star because she is greedy and bolts her food, or Cooper's Harry with his froglike mouth, or Lily with her capacity to swallow large objects without harm. All of these children display physical attributes which might explain the disappearance of the sharp trinket but they also typify the greed (Molly) and literalism (Harry and Lily) of Nokes. Finally, he promotes spiritual oldness as he condemns spiritual youngness. Because he is himself a 'burglar' – he 'stole' Alf's skill long ago by pretending it was his own – he views Alf as a burglar who probably stole the star himself, given his 'nimble' dexterity. When confronted by reality rather than its earthly shadow (when Alf appears to him as the Faery-King), he refuses to believe Alf's admission that the star came from Faërie and went to Smith. He also refuses to accept Alf's accusation that he is a 'vain old fraud' whose work was actually performed by Alf. Alf grants him the 'miracle' of transformation into a thin man but he still does not believe in the King: 'He was artful. Too nimble', he declares (p. 59), construing art and miracles to be manipulation and tricks, the devices of the burglar and the magician. Possessing free will like Smith he as freely chooses to reject the truth as Smith does to accept it when confronted by the King. He continues to suffer the effects of that pride and greed and literalism common to the *vetus homo*.

Tolkien carefully underscores the morality play of the story through the use and etymology of his characters' names. Nokes in the obsolete and rare sense, according to the *OED*, means 'a ninny' or 'fool'. Smith, as a very common surname, suggests Everyman (or an Everyman who does not mind being common, as one expression of his humility) and also the artistry of the smith who works in iron. But Alf or Elf, more than the other two characters, possesses an unusual name: in mythology the name refers to the species of supernatural beings known as 'elves'. Often implying a malicious being or demon, a succubus or incubus type of 'monster', the name can also be attributed to any diminutive creature, especially a child. Often it is a 'tricksy' (nimble?) creature, such tricks resembling the deceit implied by the etymology of the artist Niggle's name and by the burglar-artist Bilbo. Thus the three characters in 'Smith' through their names exemplify the roles of the monster-fool, the everyman-hero, and the divine or elven saviour-guide. Unlike *The Hobbit*, however, in this fairy-story it is the saviour and not the hero who 'battles' against the monster. The hero contrasts with the fool through his reaction when he encounters the saviour.

The story is appropriately structured around the journeys from one world to another: Alf's journeys into the primary world, Smith's journeys into the secondary world. Smith's journeys end when he meets the Faery-Queen on his last trip and when on the way back he meets the Faery-King, Alf. (In contrast, Nokes the Master never meets or understands the Faery-Queen, envisioned by him as a sweet cake-icing doll, and even after meeting the King many times never recognises him as king.) Thus Alf enters the *primary* world from Faërie and Smith enters the *secondary* world of Faërie from the primary world: one is an apprentice-cook in appearance and an elf-king in reality, one is a smith or artist in appearance and something far greater in reality ('The shadow was the truth', his son says, referring to the long shadow he cast upon one return from Faërie). Alf's roles as cook and king remind us of the Christian concept of the Incarnation of the divine Word in mortal flesh in Christ: he submerges his nobility beneath the humble guise of cook's help. Smith's role as artist allows him to journey to Faërie like the Christian's soul journeying to the Celestial City, the Holy Jerusalem where he eventually meets Christ the King. His passport from one world to the other is the star that allows him to be called Starbrow in reality and that signals his rebirth or recovery like the star announcing the rebirth of man in the birth of Christ. Alf's passport is his cooking ability, which suggests familiarity with the needs of the body rather than the soul, unlike Smith's.

Cooking provides physical sustenance and in itself is neither good nor bad. It thus serves a double symbolic purpose in this story. As Wootton Major is known for the excellence of its cooking, it is an appropriate place to test man's values. Material good can become an end in itself, which can subvert the soul, in the medieval sense. So the Master Cook occupies the most important symbolic role: as the agent of life he functions as a liaison between the material and spiritual realms and this world and the other world of Faërie, because with his artistry and skill he can satisfy both the spirit and body of his fellow man. Alf the messenger to man like the Word of God brings Good News with him in his artistry – and 'mortality' – as a cook, that which Smith in his elaborate and beautiful ironwork emulates. Like Christ eventually Alf must relinquish his mortality and his sojourn in the primary world in order to return to Heaven (Faërie) as Smith must relinquish his name Starbrow and his own star in order to return to the primary world.

Smith's visits to Faërie eventually earn him Epiphany. In this case it is not the appearance of the Star of the King to the Magi but the 'appearance' of the Queen and King to Smith and his recognition of them. In effect he sees the reality beneath the surface appearance and experiences true Escape, Recovery, and Consolation. If the King represents by analogy the Christian King, then the

Queen by analogy represents the essence of Faërie suggested by sub-creation. Imagination and Love: the cardinal principles of Faërie stand revealed.

The Faery-Queen was envisioned by Nokes as a doll of sugar icing and interpreted as 'a tricky little creature' (p. 20) so unscrupulous that she might not allow each of the twenty-four children to receive a trinket in the slice of Great Cake – only 'if the Fairy Queen plays fair' (p. 20). What seems tricksy and manipulative to Nokes seems artistic and alive to Smith, who swallows the fairy star. Every twenty-four years, or every generation, there exists a single child (or 'reader') capable of receiving the fairy star and recognising the Faery-Queen. The gift of the star acknowledges Smith's appreciation of Faërie and also his artistic talent; it allows him to escape ('Escape') from the primary world into the secondary world of Faërie. The escape occurs in two ways: first, Smith actually transports himself into the other world of Faërie, another country, another world. But also this 'reader' becomes himself an artist or a sub-creator and provides escape for others. Hence, on his tenth birthday he begins to 'grow up' or mature spiritually and artistically by suddenly singing a beautiful song of Faërie. Then as smith he fashions both those 'plain and useful' objects needed by the people of the village and also beautiful iron objects wrought into 'wonderful forms that looked as light and delicate as a spray of leaves and blossom' (p. 23). Like Niggle he creates a leaf-like object: his art imitates Nature and its life.

His progress in art and in understanding – his recovery (or 'Recovery') of insight – parallels the progress of his journeys into Faërie. At first he walks quietly along the outer peripheries, then he proceeds farther into Faërie as time passes. He sees the elven mariners returning from battle at the Dark Marches in a terrifying vision which compels him to turn away from the sea and the strand and toward the safer, inner Kingdom of Faërie. Faërie seems to embody in its life-forms the mirror image of the strong iron leaf and flower objects he creates: the King's Tree consists of 'tower upon tower, into the sky, and its light was like the sun at noon; and it bore at once leaves and flowers and fruits uncounted, and not one was the same as any other that grew on the Tree' (p. 28). Life *is* art in Faërie. Both provide a recovery, physical and spiritual, for Smith. Note that he once encounters a lake of water unlike any natural lake he has ever seen, for it is 'harder than stone and sleeker than glass', with flame and fiery creatures circling below.

This unnatural lake is also a deathlike and death-dealing artifact: when he falls on it a Wind 'roaring like a great beast' hurls him away. He is saved by a birch, a natural object of life and life-giving power antithetical to the deadly lake, which saves him at the cost of its own leaves: it wept, and 'tears fell from its branches like rain. He set his hand upon its white bark saying, "Blessed be the birch! What can I do to make amends or give thanks?"' (p. 30). The birch suggests a tree of life like the Tree of Life whose spirit of rebirth and Recovery pervades fantasy for Tolkien.

Thus he creates iron leaves and flowers of beauty and practical domestic implements, but never weapons of war. He understands through the recovery of perspective or insight the difference between death and life, our world and Faërie. Knowing that the evils of Faërie must be combated by weapons too dangerous for mortals, he knows also that 'he could have forged weapons that in his own world would have had power enough to become the matter of great tales and be worth a king's ransom', even though in Faërie they would have received little notice. Hence always in his sojourns he acts as a 'learner and explorer, not a warrior' (p. 24).

Eventually he earns not only Escape and partial Recovery but full Recovery and rebirth as well as Consolation or Joy. He 'sees' the Faery-Queen, although he does not recognise her in the first incident; and then he understands her and what she represents in the second, in both incidents experiencing joy and consolation. First appearing as 'a young maiden with flowing hair and a kilted skirt', she laughs and smiles at him while she chastises him for venturing here without the queen's permission. Joining with her in a dance, he experiences 'the swiftness and the power and the joy to accompany her' – the joy or consolation of Faërie incarnate in fantasy, in effect (p. 33). The dance as an art form in itself suggests the paradox of art conjoined with nature, art *alive*. So she lends him the symbol of Faërie, a Living Flower which will never die. It emblematises the eternal life of art like the flowers and leaves adorning the King's Tree and the 'blessed birch'. In the second encounter she appears as a queen, but without a crown or throne, who wears a host glimmering like 'the stars above' and a white flame burning on her head (pp. 36–7). This time she communicates with him without words. At first ashamed of Nokes' image of her, he is reminded by her, 'Better a little doll, maybe, than no memory of Faery at all'. Then to pinpoint the rebirth or recovery of vision possible to the explorer of Faërie, she declares, 'For some the only glimpse. For some the awaking' (p. 37). *Seeing* the doll-queen has allowed him to *awaken*, to be reborn and Recover. And when she touches his head, he experiences simultaneously primary-world sorrow coupled with secondary-world joy: 'he seemed to be both in the World and in Faery, and also outside them and surveying them, so that he was at once in bereavement, and in ownership, and in peace' (p. 38). Once the 'stillness' passes in a moment of joy and peace, he must return to the 'bereavement' of the world.

Having returned to the 'world', however, Smith must give up his star, signalling Epiphany; to the King. His quest is complete. But because this is itself a fairy-story, its ending also bestows a eucatastrophe upon its reader (who, like Smith, must return at *its* end to the bereavement of the world). Smith chooses the great-grandson of Nokes to be the next recipient of the star, and he and we now know that at least for those graced with goodness and imagination the future holds the possibility of journey to Faërie. The star resembles in this moral sense the Living Flower of art. The story ends with yet another great Feast of Good Children, as it has begun, and after yet another child, a 'New Man', has been picked to continue artistic endeavours.

A new 'son' will some day meet his spiritual parents, or the King and Queen of Faërie that is, of the secondary world embodied in fantasy, just as at the end the old father Smith returns to his physical family in the primary world and leaves his artistic heir Tim to the joy of Faërie. The fairy-story concerns cycles temporal and spatial – the passing of one generation to another, the journey from one world to another. Nokes allows Alf to inherit his vocational role as Master Cook, Smith allows his son to inherit his vocational role as Smith (once he too was Smithson), and Smith and Alf both allow Tim to inherit his former role as artist, explorer of Faërie. Construction and creativity, whether material or imaginative, foster the continuation of such natural cycles; destruction denies life, perpetrates death, both materially and spiritually. It is the warrior, especially the Germanic lord, who for Tolkien most frequently occupies the polar opposite of the human artist and the Christian king. In his medieval parodies such a lord kills and maims, and destroys civilisation out of a murderous self-aggrandisement. He represents a Nokes with power – and with weapons. He represents as well a very medieval but very human monster – the Germanic king. We turn now to Tolkien's medieval parodies, the formal antitheses of his Christian fairy-stories.

4 The Germanic King: Tolkien's Medieval Parodies

The medieval parodies differ in genre or form and theme from Tolkien's earlier creative and critical efforts. Neither lecture, children's story, nor fairy-story, they consist of lay, romance and *fabliau*, alliterative-verse drama, 'imram', and lyric. Such genres specifically derive from the Middle Ages. 'The Lay of Aotrou and Itroun' is modelled upon the Breton lay of the twelfth to the fourteenth centuries characteristic of northern France but influenced by old Celtic tales.[1] *Farmer Giles of Ham* combines the late medieval forms of the *fabliau* and the romance.[2] 'The Homecoming of Beorhtnoth Beorhthelm's Son' functions as an alliterative-verse drama continuation of the Old English heroic poem 'The Battle of Maldon'.[3] 'Imram' as an English poetic reworking of the Latin prose *Navigatio Sancti Brendani Abbatis* parodies the medieval Irish genre of the voyage (or 'imram').[4] Finally *The Adventures of Tom Bombadil* in its sixteen poems includes some lyrics strongly influenced by Old English principles of scansion. As a whole it cannot be termed medieval parody because, granted its supposed derivation from the hobbit records in the Red Book of Westmarch, it relates to Middle-earth instead of to the Middle Ages.[5]

The chief difference between these medieval parodies and Tolkien's other works resides then in their formally mimetic nature. It is true that *The Hobbit* and *The Lord of the Rings* rely heavily upon medieval ideas and works for their shape and structure, and their meaning.[6] It is also true that the fairy-story form of 'Leaf by Niggle' and 'Smith of Wootton Major' springs from and is heavily influenced by the Christian ethos predominant during the Middle Ages. However, a second and related difference involves Tolkien's distinction between the elegy, or Drama, and Literature, made in the lectures on *Beowulf* and on fairy-stories. Possibly with the exception of *Farmer Giles of Ham* these medieval parodies might all be characterised as elegies similar to *Beowulf*. Tolkien defined the latter as an heroic-elegiac poem because 'all its first 3,136 lines are the prelude to a dirge: *him þa gegiredan Geata leode ad ofer eorðan unwaclicne* [then the people of the Geats made ready for him a splendid pyre on the earth]'.[7] Distinguishing the elegy from the fantasy in his lecture on fairy-stories, Tolkien shows that the elegy, like the Drama, offers a dyscatastrophe common to the primary world with its mutability and death in contrast to the fantasy's eucatastrophe common to the secondary world with its Joy, Consolation, and Recovery.[8] All of the medieval parodies stress the difficulty of living in this primary (or real) world, whether England (Maldon, the Little Kingdom) or Ireland. So also all of them, with the exception of 'The Lay', a poem whose time-period remains difficult to date precisely, refer to periods or events historical or legendary occurring during the Middle Ages. *Farmer Giles* has as its subject a pre-Arthurian time (that is, before A.D. 600) but has as its imaginary author a fourteenth-century writer similar to the *Gawain* poet. 'The Homecoming' pinpoints its time as exactly A.D. 991, the date of the Battle of Maldon. 'Imram' deals with the last, legendary, voyage of St Brendan in the years 565–73. In contrast *The Hobbit* and *The Lord of the Rings* reflect a fantasy- or secondary-world existent only in the imagination; and the fairy-stories trace the relationship between a primary and secondary world of which the latter, as Faërie, bears a strong resemblance to the Christian Other World. Further, all these elegiac works are imbued with a sadness that distinguishes them from the joyful, eucatastrophic fairy-stories and the happily-ended *Hobbit* and 'New Hobbit'. 'The Lay' as an explicitly elegiac poem nears its end with these words: 'Sad is the note and sad the lay, / but mirth we meet not every day' (p. 266). While *Farmer Giles* seems superficially to end happily, in fact its conclusion masks a profoundly disturbing realisation about the cyclical nature of the reigns of kings and the sway of Fortune in this world, almost medieval in its similarity to the tragic stories of the fall of princes in Chaucer's *Monk's Tale* or to the medieval tragedy caused by the turn of Fortune's wheel in his *Troilus and Criseyde*.[9] 'Homecoming' ends with monks chanting the Office of the Dead to mourn the death of Beorhtnoth. 'Imram' concludes with the cold grim reminder that St Brendan died 'under a rain-clad sky, / journeying whence no ship returns; / and his bones in Ireland lie' (p. 1561). Even St Brendan's last words to his monastic brother can hardly be characterised as joyful in their admonishing tone: if the latter wants to know more about this paradisal land, 'in a boat then, brother, far afloat / you must labour in the sea, / and find for yourself things out of mind: / you will learn no more of me' (p. 1561). Learning and labour for the Christian remain arduous tasks. These stern endings differ radically from the cheery 'Well, I'm back' of Sam at the end of the trilogy and the laughing 'Thank goodness' of Bilbo in *The Hobbit*. That cheeriness belongs only to the secondary world of fantasy.

What interests Tolkien in these medieval parodies in lieu of that spatial journey from a primary to a secondary world in the fairy-story or within a secondary world in *The Hobbit* and *The Lord of the Rings* is the temporal shift from one phase to another in the United Kingdom's past. In a broader sense the passage of time, change, has always interested Tolkien: Bilbo and Frodo mature in microcosm as, in macrocosm, Middle-earth moves from its Third to its Fourth Age. The maturation of Niggle and Smith in the fairy-stories transcends the merely chronological passage of years. But in the medieval parodies the protagonist does not grow either chronologically or spiritually so much as degenerate, fall, or die – like the knight in 'The Lay', King Augustus in *Farmer Giles*, Beorhtnoth in 'Homecoming', and the questing St Brendan in 'Imram'. Further, these negative changes mark a time of dramatic change in the macrocosm, defined either as a family in 'The Lay', a kingdom in *Farmer Giles*, a nation in 'Homecoming', or the Christian community in 'Imram'. That is, in 'The Lay' the father's desire for an heir leads to his wife's pregnancy, the birth of twins, his death followed by hers, then the end of his line and the ruin of his castle fiefdom. The fall of Augustus Bonifacius's old kingdom and the rise of Giles's new kingdom alters considerably the countryside and its community. The change of an older Germanic-heroic culture to a newer romantic-chivalric and more Christian one is imminent in 'Homecoming'. Finally, in 'Imram' the dialogue between monks of different generations (the 'father' Brendan and his younger 'brother') heightens the passage of one age (the age of paganism that regards the other world as elven) to another (the age of Christianity that regards the other world as Christian) in the sixth century.

The child, nephew, or heir who matures into the hero dominates many of Tolkien's greatest descriptions of a secondary world; as we have seen previously, the child symbolises the New Man or *novus homo*. In contrast the old man, uncle, father, representative of a dying culture, occupies the head of the household or the head of state in a primary world setting such as England or Ireland. It is this figure Tolkien observes in the medieval parodies through the role of the knight or the king. The child, nephew, or heir occupies a complementary role, either literally as the king's heir or more figuratively as his subordinate warrior, knight, or servant. In every case his attempt to revitalise the community or culture dominated by the old knight or king fails or is marked by frustration and stultification. This occurs not through any fault of his own so much as through the debilitating consequences of the old king's behaviour.

I. *'Ofermod'*: The Medieval King

Tolkien outlines his conclusions concerning medieval ideas of kingship in the short third part of 'The Homecoming' entitled *'Ofermod'*. Using Beorhtnoth as an example of the bad lord, he specifies his chief flaw as *ofermod*, Old English for 'pride'. In lines 89–90 of 'The Battle of Maldon', the Old English poet explains the reason for the loss of the battle: ða se eorl ongan for his ofermode alyfan landes to fela laþere ðeode, or 'then the earl in his overmastering pride actually yielded ground to the enemy, as he should not have done' (p. 19). Because the *comitatus* ethic pervasive in Old English heroic poetry defined the lord's chief obligation to his tribe of warriors as that of wise leadership, protection from enemies, and food, shelter, and reward for valour in battle, such folly destroys the earl himself and most of his tribe. The reason for Beorhtnoth's pride is simple: 'Yet this element of pride,. in the form of the desire for honour and glory, in life and after death, tends to grow, to become a chief motive, driving a man beyond the bleak heroic necessity to excess – to chivalry' (p. 20). When a chief considers his men as a means to the end of self-glorification he suffers from the pride characteristic, according to Tolkien at least, of chivalry. Such excessive pride is not truly indicative of heroism. Beowulf, like

Beorhtnoth, finds criticism from Tolkien because of his error in judgement in fighting the Dragon alone, a man of fifty guilty of the same overweening pride. 'He will not deign to lead a force against the dragon, as wisdom might direct even a hero to do; for, as he explains in a long "vaunt", his many victories have relieved him of fear' (p. 21). Boasting he will rely only on a sword and on none of his subordinates, he nevertheless fails to kill the Dragon alone and to lead his tribe wisely. It is his warrior Wiglaf who finally helps him vanquish the Dragon; but even this act of heroism, rather than *chivalry*, cannot save the leaderless tribe doomed to fall before the onslaughts of the Swedes and Frisians.

In 'The Battle of Maldon', too, the subordinate warrior portrays the positive and heroic values of love and loyalty for his lord distinguished from the chief's negative and chivalric value of *ofermod*. The old retainer Beorhtwold ready to lay down his life for his foolish lord proclaims that

> Hige sceal þe heardra, heorte þe cenre,
> mod sceal þe mare þe ure maegen lytlað.

> Will shall be the sterner, heart the bolder,
> spirit the greater as our strength lessens. (p. 5)

Such love and loyalty in Germanic heroic poems are expressed through acts of valour by a subordinate warrior; in a Christian medieval poem like *Piers Plowman* they are ultimately translated into the faith, hope, and charity represented by Abraham, Moses, and the Samaritan, all types of Christ as the *novus homo*. Tolkien anticipates this transformation without mentioning Christianity explicitly by designating for the subordinate warrior a position on the continuum at the opposite end to his lord. 'Personal pride was therefore in him at its lowest, and love and loyalty at their highest' (p. 20). What Tolkien does here, of course, is to reconcile Germanic heroic values with Christian ones in the same way as the *Beowulf* poet, if not Beowulf himself.

In the 1936 lecture on *Beowulf* Tolkien revealed its dual levels (Germanic and Christian) in the figures of its monsters. Representative on one level of the natural forces of chaos and death threatening man, on another level they signify the supernatural dangers of sin and spiritual death. Thus the monsters Beowulf fights in the poem must be destroyed externally by heroism in battle but as well they symbolically project internal flaws in the nations and their lords which can be conquered only by wisdom and self-control. In short the hero must display that *sapientia et fortitudo* characteristic of the Germanic and the Christian leader. If Beowulf fails here, Bilbo and even Frodo do not – as we have seen and will see, in the fiction published in the year after the *Beowulf* article (*The Hobbit*, 1937) and continually revised throughout the ensuing years ('The New Hobbit', 1937–49).

But in his later fictional works Tolkien's attention to the Germanic-Christian values splits. In the medieval parodies published during the years 1945 to 1955 ('The Lay', 1945; *Farmer Giles*, 1949; 'The Homecoming', 1953; 'Imram', 1955) he focuses primarily on the failure of Germanic values. In contrast, in the fairy-stories published during the equivalent period of 1945–67 ('Leaf by Niggle', 1945; 'Smith of Wootton Major', 1967) he focuses on the success of Christian values. In both groups he grows less interested in literal monsters and more interested in figurative ones. That monster in the medieval parodies assumes the familiar form of the Germanic king, chief, or master suffering from an excess of *ofermod*. (Antithetically, in the fairy-stories the king of Faërie resembles the Christian King.)

In the four works discussed in this chapter the Germanic king is depicted in various ways. In 'The Lay of Aotrou and Itroun' (1945) he is a Briton lord whose chief defect is an internal pride in his familial line which leads to his death and the loss of his family. In *Farmer Giles of Ham* (1949), however, he is a king whose pride stems from the cultural values of the aristocracy – from an external social rather than an internal spiritual source. As such, King Augustus Bonifacius resembles the proud Beorhtnoth. In asking himself why Beorhtnoth committed such a grievous error Tolkien concludes: 'Owing to a defect of character, no doubt; but a character, we may surmise, not only formed by nature, but moulded also by "aristocratic tradition", shrined in tales and verse of poets now lost save for echoes' (p. 21). So the pride and avarice of the King Augustus (the spiritual equivalent of Beorhtnoth's 'death') lead to the fall of his kingdom and the rise of the hero from the lowest of classes (remember he is a farmer). In 'The Homecoming' (1953) the *ofermod* of the Anglo-Saxon earl Beorhtnoth results in his death and those of his warriors at Maldon in 991, symbolising the demise of the Germanic heroic culture. At the end the 'Voice in the dark' (identified by Tolkien as that of the Danish king Canute) is heard admiring the monks' song; during his reign from 1016 to 1035 his Christianity allowed him to rule both Danes and English as a wise and strong king, the antithesis of the weak earl Beorhtnoth. Finally, in 'Imram' (1955) because of its medieval Irish genre and Christian subject, heroic values are expressed only metaphorically in the role of St Brendan as a knight-militant, or superior 'lord' to a youthful subordinate, in a clash of generations within a single social class – the clergy. In all four, Tolkien moves backward in time gradually. The courtly 'Lay' is followed by the mock-chivalric and very fourteenth-century *Giles*; then we encounter the late tenth century in 'The Homecoming' and the late sixth century in 'Imram'. In this last medieval parody, set earliest in time and most Christian in bias, we can detect that transition to a form and a theme with which Tolkien would end his publishing career in his final years – the fairy-story detailing the hero's journey to another world through the employment of Christian virtues, chiefly charity.

II 'The Lay of Aotrou and Itroun': the Briton Lord

'The Lay' has been termed a poem with 'an unusually strong religious cast, which transforms the customary series of knightly exploits and amours into a story of temptation and fall'.[10] But in addition and less obviously, there exists in this lay a delineation of *familial* pride in the knight Aotrou very similar to the tribal pride of Beorhtnoth resulting in the deaths of him and his warriors. If the latter abrogates his Germanic relationship with his men by using them as a means to an end the former abrogates his feudal relationship with his wife by using her as a means to an end.

   Beorhtnoth desired glory in battle in order to make immortal his name. Aotrou, imagining 'lonely age and death, his tomb / unkept, while strangers in his room / *with other names* and other shields / were masters of his halls and fields' (p. 254, my italics), yearns not for glory in battle but for a child and heir. That his situation is worsening is clear from the key lines 'his pride was empty, vain his hoard, / without an heir to land and sword' (p. 254): he resembles the old king Beowulf who, childless, faces the end of his family line and of his leaderless tribe. Tolkien's use of 'pride' here indicates he intends it in the Germanic and racial and not the Christian and spiritual sense. Where Aotrou errs, then, occurs in his use of his wife as a mere tool in implementing his ends, and in the violation of her love and loyalty to him in a subtle parody of the chivalric code.

In return for wooing and wedding her with a ring Aotrou receives her love in 'board and bed'. Tolkien likens the social bond joining lord and lady to the contract between lord and retainer by linking these two reciprocal gestures. Aotrou's economic and literal protection of the lady (the ring) complements her domestic and conjugal expressions of love (board and bed). He fails her when he finds inadequate that expression – when he yearns for a child 'his house to cheer, / to fill his courts with laughter clear' (p. 254). His failure Tolkien underscores through the monstrous or supernatural female replacements for Itroun – Corrigan the witch and the mysterious white doe which leads him to Corrigan. In effect Aotrou 'mates' with the first and hunts the second on two separate journeys, the first suggesting a perversion of the Ovidian 'soft hunt' and the second an inversion of the 'hard hunt' which medieval poets, especially Chaucer in the *Book of the Duchess*, used to depict the bifold role of the knight as courtly lover and skilful hunter in pursuing the heart/hart. That is, he symbolically depicts Aotrou as mating with the monster that his excessive familial pride or pride in his lineage has compelled him to become. Corrigan with her 'dark and piercing' eyes 'filled with lies' gives him a vial of magic fluid to rectify Aotrou's infertility, and through this he is able to father twins – and to deceive his wife as darkly as Corrigan will deceive him. He deceives her, that is, by preferring to her himself (or Corrigan the witch as monstrous *alter ego*). Specifically he deceives her by pretending the cause of the conception is natural. Suggesting a merry feast so that they 'will *feign* our love begun / in joy anew, anew to run / down happy paths' (my italics), he construes his motivation as an attempt to realise 'our hearts' desire' more quickly – but achieved because of their 'hope and prayer' and not the magic vial of Corrigan (p. 257, my italics). The word 'feign' is aptly chosen.

Throughout the 'Lay' Aotrou supposes his own desires are those of Itroun. After the twins are born his mistake becomes more apparent. Having attained an heir and proved his ability as lover Aotrou will now prove his ability as knight by journeying to fulfil his wife's least desire:

> Is 't not, fair love, most passing sweet
> the heart's desire at last to meet?

Yet if thy heart still longing hold,
or lightest wish remain untold,
that will I find and bring to thee,
though I should ride both land and sea!

(p. 259)

He pretends their children resulted from his virility as the satisfaction of her other desires will be similarly satisfied by his journeying
and chivalric questing. But what she wants is clear: 'I would not
have thee run nor ride / to-day nor ever from my side' (p. 259).
True, she expresses a desire for cold water and venison, but she
regards this as a 'foolish wish', a hunger superficial in contrast to
her need for him by her side – for his continued protection of her.
He ignores her real desire in order to hunt the white doe and
perform a chivalrous deed as he believes a true knight should. But
Tolkien describes this hunt as a 'reckless' and 'vexed' pursuit of
'deer that fair and fearless range' beyond the reach of most mortals
(p. 260). In short, his pride is excessive and, in Tolkien's pejorative
sense, chivalric.

When the white doe leads him to Corrigan and her demand for
love he violates the terms of yet another contract, in addition to the
marital one, by refusing her her fee and incurring thereby her
condemnation to 'stand as stone / and wither lifeless and alone' (p.
262) – she takes back that life-giving fertility bestowed on him by
the vial. His spiritual 'death' has already occurred; his physical one
follows in three days. The water in the vial he hoped would
rejuvenate his familial line, and also his marriage to Itroun,
becomes instead the potion of death, sterility, darkness – of
impotence, in effect. His excessive pride in himself and his desire
for glory, the perpetuation of his name, cause two deaths and,
apparently, the end of his family and his estate, granted the
'ruined toft' described in the first lines of the lay.

The real 'hero' of this lay is Itroun, the loving and loyal wife
whose subordination to her husband resembles that of the servant
or retainer to the master or king. Her death, while useless, occurs
after she learns of his and expresses so well the extent of her love
for him. If he had pursued her true desire – to remain by her side –
he might have redeemed himself: if he had understood her request
for cold water figuratively rather than literally he might have lived.
For the poem concludes with a prayer that

God keep us all in hope and prayer
from evil rede and from despair,
by *waters blest* of Christendom
to dwell, until at last we come
to joy of Heaven where is queen
the maiden Mary pure and clean.

(p. 266, my italics)

Just as the white doe leads Aotrou to Corrigan, his wife might have led him to the Virgin Mary, had he chosen to 'pursue' her. Itroun would have performed as a spiritual guide on the journey to that forest and holy fountain traditionally associated with Paradise. So she resembles Beatrice in Dante's *La Vita Nuova* and *Divine Comedy* as a guide to the Virgin Mary.

The child as heir, represented by the male and female twins, never has a chance to mature into the hero. Aotrou's vision of their laughter while they play 'on lawns of sunlight without hedge' (p. 258) is tinged with darkness – the 'dark shadow at their [hedges'] edge'. Eventually the vision disappears altogether, both for Aotrou, now dead, and also for the reader: 'and if their children lived yet long, / or played in garden hale and strong, / they saw it not, nor found it sweet / their heart's desire at last to meet' (p. 266). The only laughter remaining is 'cold and pale', springing from Broceliande's own 'homeless hills', the habitat of Corrigan. The monstrous witch as Aotrou's dark *alter ego* replaces his heir and thus denies him immortality and 'life'. The lay ends then with a dirge that mourns the deaths of lord and lady as part of the tragedy inherent in this world, and emphasises the need for man to transcend its evil through God's grace. The last line alludes fittingly to the joy of a Heaven inhabited by 'the maiden Mary pure and clean' – a miracle, a mother whose child left her still virgin, a mother whose heir redeemed and purified all of mankind unlike the heirs of Aotrou, who have disappeared without a trace. To seek a racial immortality through heirs like Aotrou reveals a folly rectified only by the quest for spiritual immortality through God's Son. Aotrou's failure is clearly attributable to the chivalric code. It is matched by that of King Augustus Bonifacius in *Farmer Giles of Ham*.

III *Farmer Giles of Ham*: **the Late Medieval English King**

Farmer Giles of Ham represents Tolkien's only medieval parody that both imitates a medieval form or genre and also burlesques medieval literary conventions, ideas, and characters drawn from fourteenth-century works, especially *Sir Gawain and the Green Knight* and Chaucer's *Canterbury Tales*. Published in 1949, it marks as well the completion of *The Lord of the Rings* and, as 'a vacation from the "things higher . . . deeper . . . darker" which these epics [*The Lord of the Rings* and *The Silmarillion*] treat',[11] spoofs the epic through its mock-heroic style and the academic scholarship of its fussy, editorial preface by the pseudo-historian and linguist who 'discovered' the original manuscript. In addition, it also mocks Tolkien's own creative works and the medieval literature from which so many of his ideas of heroism, chivalry, and kingship derive.

The mock-heroic style reduces the grandiose and long Latin title of the work to the simple translation *Farmer Giles of Ham*: the serious is made trivial. So the hero and his chief adversary become a rude farmer and his domesticated pet. Giles never wants to slay monsters; his cowardly dog barks him out of bed one night when he senses an intruder. This giant intruder turns out to be deaf and nearsighted, accidentally flattening Galatea the cow as he enters Giles's farm and mistaking his assailant's blunderbuss charge for a swarm of horseflies. The second monster, the dragon Chrysophylax, after defeat in battle becomes a large pet who, like Garm the dog earlier, protects Giles's farm and his acquired treasure. Tolkien's medievalised art undergoes a humorous reduction very similar to the squashing of Galatea, named after Pygmalion's ivory statue brought to life as a woman in the classical myth. Suggesting the lifegiving power inherent in the artist's function, the myth under mock-heroic treatment shows how life (the cow) is snuffed out by the artist (a deaf and shortsighted giant) and how myth (classical or medieval, but in this case from Ovid) is flattened into burlesque (modern, from Tolkien). Throughout *Farmer Giles* it is not the mythology of Ovid's *Metamorphoses* Tolkien delights in flattening so much as his own mythology portrayed in *The Hobbit* and 'The New Hobbit'. These works were influenced by various medieval sources, including *Beowulf*, as understood in his 'Beowulf: The Monsters and the Critics', and *Sir Gawain and the Green Knight*, later discussed in the 'Ofermod' section of 'The

Homecoming of Beorhtnoth Beorhthelm's Son'.

That is, in *The Hobbit* Tolkien fictionalised ideas of monstrosity first delineated in the *Beowulf* article. In *The Hobbit* the two primary monsters were Gollum in the first part and the dragon Smaug in the second, the first signifying the more physical sins of gluttony and sloth, the second signifying the more intellectual sins of wrath, envy, avarice, and pride. But these monsters merely externalised the evil present in Bilbo and other characters. So avarice and pride also troubled Thorin the dwarf-king and the Master of Dale, expressed through their desire for kingship or mastery over others. Finally, the critic-as-monster was represented by the supercilious adult narrator of the children's story.

Tolkien parodies this same schema in *Farmer Giles*. One important clue to his intentions exists in the use of the phrase 'until the dragon came' to mark the change in Giles's luck caused by the first appearance of the dragon (p. 22). Originally ending his *Beowulf* article, it dramatised the universal threat of chaos and death to mankind. Further, the giant who stumbles onto Giles's farm mimics the monster Grendel who deliberately attacked Heorot out of envy; the dragon Chrysophylax in the later parts who first attacks Ham and then is attacked within his lair by Giles plays the part of Beowulf's Dragon who first ravages the Geat countryside because of the theft of a cup and then is approached in his barrow by Beowulf and Wiglaf. *Farmer Giles* also invites comparison with *The Hobbit*: its first monster, Gollum, exhibits inordinate gluttony and sloth (lower, physical sins) and its second monster, Smaug, exhibits avarice and pride (higher, more spiritual sins) in the same way that the giant is physically limited because deaf and near-sighted and the dragon is spiritually limited because greedy and conscienceless. In addition the metaphor of kingship in *Farmer Giles* reiterates that of *The Hobbit*: Augustus Bonifacius is depicted as avaricious and proud as both King Beowulf and Thorin the dwarf-king. Finally, the pompous editor-translator who belittles the vulgarity of the manuscript resembles the narrator of *The Hobbit* who belittles the childishness and stupidity of the halflings and dwarves throughout.

But this fictionalisation of the *Beowulf* article differs from the original article and *The Hobbit* because it also fictionalises the distinction between heroism and chivalry evidenced four years later in 'Ofermod'. In the latter Tolkien perceives that the excessive pride of king or knight stems from the chivalric code of the aristocracy as criticised in both *Beowulf* and *Sir Gawain and the Green Knight*. In 'Ofermod' he uses these as exemplary works; in *Farmer Giles* he also introduces new material drawn from Chaucer's *Canterbury Tales*, especially the *fabliaux* of the Miller and the Reeve, to mock the heroic form of the romance. Just as the Miller tells a scatological tale to humiliate Chaucer's Knight, who has just narrated a long romance of lofty, appropriately aristocratic idealism and chivalry, so Tolkien's hero in this *fabliau*-romance, a crude farmer, will humiliate several knights and even a king. Their chivalry cannot be viewed as ideal because it distracts the aristocracy from protecting the lower classes for which it is responsible. Giles becomes a knight and then a king of his own realm because he does not fall prey to the excessive pride inherent in the chivalric code of the upper class. However, he also apparently lacks the manners and courtesy of the knight as defined in *Sir Gawain and the Green Knight*.

The testing of Sir Gawain's *courtesie* occurs on the three days he is visited by his lord's lady even while his allegiance to his host-lord and to God (through loyalty and through adherence to Christian virtue) is simultaneously tested. That he fails, even mildly, despite exemplary behaviour, becomes clear by the end of the poem when he scandalously accepts the lady's magic girdle, deceives his host by refusing to give him this 'winning' as he had promised, succumbs to cowardice in combat by flinching before the Green Knight's axe, and then blames his failure rather discourteously and rudely upon a woman. Tolkien terms the work, in 'Ofermod', 'in plain intention a criticism or valuation of a whole code of sentiment and conduct, in which heroic courage is only a part, with different loyalties to serve' (p. 23). For Sir Gawain does risk death in order to support his lord and uncle, King Arthur, literally and courageously by accepting the challenge of the Green Knight and more figuratively and spiritually by showing his loyalty and love for him. He is a heroic figure here *because* he is a subordinate.

Tolkien deliberately invokes *Sir Gawain and the Green Knight* in *Farmer Giles* through humorous parallels. Specifically, the entry of the 'rude and uncultured' giant (p. 10) into Giles's territory at the beginning mimics the boisterous arrival of the Green Knight – atop his green horse – in the midst of the king's Christmas feast. Unknowingly this giant does issue a 'challenge' to the incipient knight Giles similar to that of the Green Knight – for thereafter

Giles finds himself embroiled in knightly exploits fighting the dragon with the subsequent reward of the king's sword 'Tailbiter' for his valour. Later in the work there is actually a Christmas feast during which the dragon, lured to the territory by the giant's idea that knights have become mythical, is ravaging the countryside as a rude 'guest'. And the king's knights, who in their cowardice resemble Arthur's, delay in fighting this dragon because of a tournament planned for St John's Day: 'It was obviously unreasonable to spoil the chances of the Midland Knights by sending their best men off on a dragon-hunt before the tournament was over' (p. 28). Like Sir Gawain, Giles must defend his king's honour.

More generally the theme of the two works appears similar. When manners and etiquette supersede heroic courage and loyalty to lord, then a culture has become corrupt in the worst and most effetely chivalric sense. Augustus' knights have become literalists in their interpretation of the chivalric code: they are more interested in how they appear on the outside than in what they really are on the inside. When the king acknowledges Giles's retention of 'the ancient courage of our race' his knights meanwhile talk 'among themselves about the new fashion in hats' (p. 50). Forced to accompany Giles on his quest of the dragon's lair they do not see dragon-marks on the trail because they 'were discussing points of precedence and etiquette, and their attention was distracted' (pp. 57–8). Of course they turn tail and run when confronted by the monster.

The king too seems to regard manners as more important than morals, just as he regards money as a greater good than love and loyalty. When Giles does not come to the king after being summoned upon his return with the treasure from the dragon's lair, the king scolds, 'Your manners are unfit for our presence, . . . but that does not excuse you from coming when sent for' (p. 70). Yet the king himself reacts very coarsely when he first learns of Giles's recalcitrance: his 'rage exploded', he 'bellowed', he ordered Giles to be thrown into prison (p. 69), and later he even demands the return of his gift of Tailbiter (p. 70). Indeed, his greatest concern throughout the tale lies with the treasure rather than with Giles's bravery in battle: his 'knight' becomes a means to a financial end. The dragon's promise to return with his treasure after his defeat by Giles 'deeply moved' the king – 'for various reasons, not the least being financial' (p. 49). And when the beast does not reappear on the designated day Augustus rages because 'the King wanted money' (p. 53). Caring only about his coffers he fails to treat Giles as a real person; such a failure results in his kingdom's downfall.

The well-mannered and fashionable knights and king in the tale contrast with the 'rude and uncultured' giant and the merchant-like dragon who bargains with Giles over the price of his defeat – and with the coarse Farmer Giles. But the apparent heroes are revealed as adversaries and the 'monsters' becomes heroes (or the hero's pets) by the tale's end. Tolkien condemns the aristocracy throughout for its perpetration of the dehumanising chivalric code and applauds the commons' heroic courage and love which eventually triumphs over the former. Worthiness springs from good deeds and not fine clothes or ancestry or manners.

Giles, despite his uncouth behaviour, does manifest heroism and courage. The dragon immediately recognises his true nature during their first meeting: 'You have concealed your honourable name and pretended that our meeting was by chance; yet you are plainly a knight of high lineage. It used, sir, to be the custom of knights to issue a challenge in such cases, after a proper exchange of titles and credentials' (p. 43). He is actually what a knight *should be*, despite his lack of a title. Tolkien agrees with the dragon by providing an appropriate feast-day for the confrontation between hero and monster, the Feast of the Epiphany on Twelfth Night, or 6 January, when Christ was revealed to the Magi. The 'epiphany' or revelation here introduces the true knight to the dragon – and to the reader.

As the true hero of the work is a churl so its real form or genre emerges as the low-styled, humorous *fabliau* which Chaucer's Miller uses to *quyten* (or 'repay') the high-flown rhetoric of the Knight in his philosophical romance. The style of the former involves a 'bourgeois realism' in contrast to the 'aristocratic ideal-ism' of the latter.[12] So, in *Farmer Giles*, the villagers speak a rough and idiomatic language very unlike that of the genteel and elegant aristocrats. And indeed these rural folk who establish themselves as Draconarii in league with Giles derive their identities in part from Chaucer's low-life and poor Canterbury pilgrims. Not only is there Farmer Giles, reminiscent of the Miller, there is also a reeve who is as antagonistic toward Giles as Oswald is toward the Miller in the *Canterbury Tales*. The parson seems to combine Chaucer's gentle and good Parson with his learned Clerk, for he acts also as a grammarian in *Farmer Giles* and reveals the original name of

Tailbiter as Caudimordax. Finally, there exists a blacksmith who favours Giles's cause by providing him with steel chain mail and helmet, possibly a pale shadow of the blacksmith in the *Miller's Tale* who gives Absolon the hot coulter with which to 'battle' with his adversary, *hende* Nicholas, as the latter plays his crude joke for the last time.

Tolkien's view of the subordinate as more admirable than the chief or king who employs his men as instruments to boost his name in battle is expressed in this *fabliau*-romance through a class struggle between the commons and the aristocracy: the *comitatus* ethic dividing Germanic society into subordinate warriors and king is metamorphosed into that division of late medieval society into two if not three estates (usually commons, clergy, and aristocracy). The triumph of commons over aristocracy, however, communicates a singularly unmedieval and very modern idea: it suggests a nineteenth- or twentieth-century revolutionary outlook, except that the leader of the commoners actually becomes king, and a new aristocracy is created, presumably with its own new commons (note that when Giles becomes king the blacksmith engages in undertaking, the miller, given the royal monopoly on milling, serves the crown, and the parson advances to bishop). The old order is revitalised but perhaps there is no real change, except in the introduction of a bourgeoisie, yet another class. A similar consequence of the failure of the aristocratic code occurs after the death of Beorhtnoth in a work that deals with an even earlier medieval period – 'The Homecoming', describing the events of 991.

IV 'The Homecoming of Beorhtnoth Beorhthelm's Son': the Anglo-Saxon King

In this alliterative-verse drama a young man, Torthelm, a freeman and the minstrel's son, and an old man, Tidwald the *ceorl*, search the battlefield at Maldon for the body of the dead Beorhtnoth to take to the monks of Ely. The young man in his idealism views the scene from a Germanic heroic stance; the old man in his pragmatic realism views it from a pre-Christian, moralistic stance. Their dialogue functions allegorically as a debate over the merits of the two views.

Torhthelm sings of Beorhtnoth as a prince among men:

His head was higher than the helm of kings
With heathen crowns, his heart keener
and his soul clearer than swords of heroes
polished and proven; than plated gold
his worth was greater. From the world has
passed a prince peerless in peace and war,
just in judgment, generous-handed
as the golden lords of long ago.

(p. 9)

But the shrewd Tidwald recognises the true nature of this excessively proud *eorl*: he risked and lost the lives of his men to obtain
greater glory. 'Our lord was at fault, . . . / Too proud, too princely!
But his pride's cheated, . . . / He let them cross the causeway, so
keen was he / to give minstrels matter for mighty songs. /
Needlessly noble' (p. 14).

Neither of these men belongs to the aristocracy: Torhthelm,
although a freeman, is a minstrel's son and Tidwald is a farmer.
Yet Torhthelm dreams of serving his lord as a warrior in battle – 'I
loved him no less than any lord with him; / and a poor freeman
may prove in the end / more tough when tested than titled earls /
who count back their kin to kings ere Woden' (p. 8) – despite
Tidwald's admonition that iron has, in reality, a 'bitter taste', and
that, when faced with the choice, often a shieldless man is tempted
to flee rather than die for his lord. Too, Tidwald implicitly criticises
the aristocracy when he complains of the lot of the poor. The heroic
earls die in battle, but poets sing their praises in lays. In contrast,
'When the poor are robbed / and lose the land they loved and toiled
on, / they must die and dung it. No dirge for them, / and their
wives and children work in serfdom' (p. 15). This pair functions in
microcosm as those representative poor ignored by the aristocracy
and the minstrels.

Torhthelm perhaps learns something from old Tidwald on the
journey back to the monks' abbey at Ely. In a dream of darkness he
sees a lighted house and hears voices singing. The joyful song
(taken from the speech of the old retainer in 'The Battle of Maldon')
celebrates the love and loyalty of the subordinate rather than the
pride of the lord:

Heart shall be the bolder, harder be purpose,
more proud the spirit as our power lessens!

Mind shall not falter nor mood waver,
though doom shall come and dark conquer.

(p. 17)

By switching emphasis from lord to followers Torhthelm reaffirms
those values of love and loyalty to Lord celebrated as well by
Christianity that will make possible a transition from a dying
Germanic culture to a newly-flourishing Christian one.

Yet it is only 991: 'The Battle of Maldon', in terms of its criticism
of the chivalric and praise of the heroic, as Tolkien admits in
'Ofermod', occupies a chronologically medial position between the
early Beowulf and the later Sir Gawain and the Green Knight. The date
marks not only the ending of heroism but the beginning of the
triumph of chivalry, set within the context of a Christianity more
pervasive than that in the time of Beowulf (seventh–eighth century). Tolkien emphasises this transition through the use of verse
in the drama. The verse spoken by Torhthelm and Tidwald – 'I've
watched and waited, till the wind sighing / was like words whis-
pered by waking ghosts' (p. 6) – bears four stresses per line, three
of which are linked by alliteration like Old English verse. This
changes to rhyming verse (a measure predominant in France in the
thirteenth and fourteenth centuries) spoken somewhat anachronis-
tically here by a 'Voice in the dark' who comments upon the
'Dirige' of the monks at the end: 'Sadly they sing, the monks of Ely
isle! / Row men, row! Let us listen here / a while!' (p. 18). The voice
presages events of the future (the lines from the Historia Eliensis
actually refer to Canute, ruler of England from 1016 to 1035).

Sound is important in this drama, which should be staged to be
fully understood. It dramatises the change in a culture from the
primarily Germanic to the Christian through the contrast between
human words and the Word made flesh, and between the chaotic
noise of life and the silence of death. It begins with the sound of a
man moving and breathing in the darkness; it ends with the sound
of the monks' dirge as it 'fades into silence' (p. 18). The first line
introduces a suspicious voice crying 'Halt!' in the dark but in the
last lines an admiring voice urges his rowers on in order to listen to
the monks. Mostly, however, the heroic lay of Torhthelm contrasts
with the Christian service of the monks.

The flawed human lord Beorhtnoth who sacrifices his men to his
pride also contrasts with the good Lord Christ who sacrifices
himself for his 'men'. So the title of 'The Homecoming' refers

specifically to the coming home of the corpse of the dead earl but also alludes more generally to the 'homecoming' of the soul to its heavenly habitat. Thus the Office of the Dead at the end of 'The Homecoming' asks that the Lord 'Guide my way . . . into your presence' ('Dirige, Domine, in conspectu tuo viam meam'), and further, into his 'house' or temple: 'Introibo in domum tuam: adorabo ad templum / sanctum tuum in timore tuo' (p. 18). The homecoming of the true subordinate (the Christian) is joyous because he relies solely on the Lord; the homecoming of the false lord (the proud earl) is funereal because he relied too heavily on himself. The notion of return here echoes Tolkien's usage in *The Hobbit* ('There, and Back Again') and in *The Lord of the Rings*: it usually signifies redemptive change and rebirth. Because of the chivalric code, however, this literal 'return' ends only in death and darkness.

Yet there is hope. When Torhthelm ('Bright Helmet'), whose name invokes Germanic heroic values of an earlier period, fancies a barrow or pyre in the best heathen fashion for Beorhtnoth, Tidwald chides him realistically that 'Beorhtnoth we bear not Béowulf here: / no pyres for him, nor piling of mounds; / and the gold will be given to the good abbot' (p. 11). His name, meaning 'Time-Forest', intimates his awareness of time and his earth-bound values. Less imaginative and idealistic than his companion, he also advances a common-sense charity antithetical to the Germanic bloodlust of Torhthelm. When they hear corpse-robbers moving around the bodies Torhthelm wishes to 'thrash the villain' (p. 13) but the wise Tidwald cautions, 'Their life's wretched, / but why kill the creatures, or crow about it? / There are dead enough around' (p. 12). Like Gandalf counselling pity and mercy in *The Lord of the Rings*, he views homicide as destructive and evil, not heroic. He sees these corpse-strippers as hungry and masterless men deserving of pity.

But neither is Tidwald altogether Christian in his viewpoint. His *contemptus mundi* suggests a pre-Christian attitude transitionally similar to Torhthelm's post-Germanic-heroic attitude at the end of the drama. Note that he imagines the next morning as without hope: 'more labour and loss till the land's ruined; / ever work and war till the world passes' (p. 17). His is the harsh First Voice of 'Leaf by Niggle' which sought to measure justly by the Law or the demanding voice of Parish seeking practical aid and materials from his neighbour Niggle. A *tertium quid* between the artist-minstrel and the gardener-farmer or between the Germanic-heroic and the pre-Christian is announced by a 'third voice' from the future belonging, appropriately, to a warrior and a Christian, a Dane and an Englishman, a king and a lover of music.[13] Canute as a Danish king ruling England from 1016 to 1035 commands both hard labour and also enjoyment of art: 'Row men, row! Let us listen here a while.'

The *tertium quid* is symbolically enhanced by light-dark imagery. The monks' candles provide some light in the darkness to brighten the way for those journeying home, unlike the lanterns of Tidwald and Torhthelm lighting their search for corpses but similar to the hearth-light warming the dark for the loyal warriors of Torhthelm's dream vision. Both forms of light provide hopeful consolation for man doomed to live in this primary world. True, Torhthelm's way leads eventually to darkness: as Tidwald reminds us, 'dark is over all, and dead is master' (p. 17). But all ends in silence anyway, like this verse drama. Only in the Other World do light and true vision occur: the Office of the Dead asks that the Lord lead man into his presence or his *vision* ('in conspectu tuo').

The dialogue between artist and farmer here suggests the conflict between Niggle and Parish in 'Leaf by Niggle' or even Frodo and Sam in *The Lord of the Rings*. Like the divided self of Bilbo as both Took and Baggins, the complementary pair also personifies the relationship between soul and body or between the *novus* and the *vetus homo*. As the young monk and the older 'saint militant' the latter couple resurfaces with even more Christian effect in 'Imram'.

V 'Imram': the Saint Militant

Like Beorhtnoth, St Brendan must return home, but 'to find the grace to die' (p. 1561) after performing heroically on his journey-quest for the Living Land. Mostly the results of his 'voyage' (as the poem is entitled) are described to a younger monastic brother who wants easy answers but who is told to 'find for yourself things out of mind'. The 'king' here is no king at all but a Christian saint functioning as a knight-errant in his search for the home of Elvenkind, who is modelled upon the *miles Christi* described in Ephesians 6. The only mention of kingship occurs when St Brendan describes the shoreless mountain stretching into the

Cloud and resting on 'the foundered land / where the kings of kings lie low'. The 'kings of kings' are mere mortals destined to die despite their desire for glory on earth, in contrast to this errant-monk's desire for the glory of the other world 'whence no ship returns' – even though his physical remains, like theirs, reside on earth ('his bones in Ireland lie').

As a saint he most resembles the Christian king found in the fairy-story, even though this short 'imram' represents a parody of the medieval Irish genre and hence *should* invite comparison with the other medieval parodies. Its Christian message imparts the necessity for each man to become a saint-militant, to journey on his own quest of the Living Land. Its Christian hero reveals a humility in his failure of memory and strange lassitude hardly characteristic of the proud king or knight of the medieval parody. Its paradise with the Christian symbols of Tree and Star is, as Paul Kocher has suggested, equivalent to the Living Land of Elvenkind described in the mythology of Middle-earth.

But other elements suggest that the poem must be construed as a hybrid, a transitional work combining aspects of the medieval parody and the fairy-story. After all, the knight-errant in this parody is actually a saint. The elegiac ending focusing on St Brendan's death should mark it as 'drama' in Tolkien's terms, like other medieval parodies; but the work also includes a consoling vision of a secondary world usually found in the fantasy of 'literature' or the fairy-story. But most of all it contrasts a real place in the primary world (Ireland) of the past, usually described only in the parody, with the fantastic land of the other world in its eternal present, usually described only in the fairy-story. Note that this contrast is bolstered by the iconography of the landscapes: the 'loud' waves near Ireland are juxtaposed with 'silence like dew' falling 'in that isle, / and holy it seemed to be'; the 'tower tall and grey / the knell of Clúain-ferta's bell / was tolling in green Galway' is juxtaposed with the spire which is 'lit with a living fire' and 'tall as a column in High Heaven's hall, / its roots were deep as Hell' on the ancient land where 'the kings of kings lie low'; finally, the 'wood and mire' and 'clouded moon' in the 'rain-clad sky' of Ireland are juxtaposed with a paradisal white fair Tree with its white birds and surrounding fair flowers redolent of a smell 'as sweet and keen as death / that was borne upon the breeze'. As a hybrid synthesis of genres and Christian-Germanic themes it invites comparison with that greatest of Tolkienian works fusing

together in complex orchestration all the motifs and ideas concern-
ing kingship and lordship discussed in this study. In this sense
'Imram' functions as an appropriate transition to *The Lord of the
Rings*.

5 The Lord of the Rings: Tolkien's Epic

The epic form has proved useful in reflecting the clash of value systems during periods of transition in literary history. In the Old English *Beowulf* Germanic heroism conflicts with Christianity: the chivalric pride of the hero can become the excessive *superbia* condemned in Hrothgar's moralistic sermon. Similar conflicts occur in other epics or romance-epics: between the chivalric and the Christian in the twelfth-century German *Nibelungenlied* and in Sir Thomas Malory's fifteenth-century *Morte d'Arthure*, between the classical and the Christian in the sixteenth-century *Faerie Queene* of Sir Edmund Spenser, and between chivalric idealism and modern realism in the late sixteenth-century Spanish epic-novel of Cervantes, *Don Quixote*. Tolkien's *Lord of the Rings* delineates a clash of values during the passage from the Third Age of Middle-earth dominated by the elves to the Fourth Age dominated by man. Such values mask very medieval notions of Germanic heroism and Christianity evidenced earlier by Tolkien in his *Beowulf* article.

In this sense *The Lord of the Rings* resembles *The Hobbit* which, as we have seen previously, must acknowledge a great thematic and narrative debt to the Old English epic, even though *The Hobbit*'s happy ending renders it closer to fantasy in Tolkien's definition than to the elegy with its tragic ending. The difference between them stems from form: the children's story narrated by the arrogant adult in *The Hobbit* has 'grown up' sufficiently to require no fictionalised narrator in the text itself and a more expansive and flexible genre like the epic. Indeed, Randel Helms notes that we have in *The Hobbit* and its sequel what is in fact the same story, told first very simply, and then again, very intricately. Both works have the same theme, a quest on which a most unheroic hobbit achieves heroic stature; they have the same structure, the 'there and back again' of the quest romance, and both extend the quest through the cycle of one year, *The Hobbit* from spring to spring, the *Rings* from fall to fall.[1]

Although Helms does not mention their relationship with medieval ideas or even with the *Beowulf* article, still, given this reworking of a theme used earlier in *The Hobbit*, *The Lord of the Rings* must also duplicate many medieval ideas from *The Hobbit* and elsewhere in Tolkien.

As an epic novel it constitutes then a *summa* of Tolkien's art – a full development of themes originally enunciated in the *Beowulf* article and fictionalised later in other works. It was, after all, begun in 1937 – the same year *The Hobbit* was published and a year later than the *Beowulf* article – and completed in 1949, prior to the publication of many of the fairy-stories (1945–67) and the medieval parodies (1945–62). Its medial position in Tolkien's career indicates how its author might have articulated his major ideas generally and comprehensively in this mammoth work before delving into their more specialised aspects in the later fairy-stories and parodies.

As a synthesis then of Tolkienian ideas, both Germanic heroic or medieval and Christian, it reconciles value systems over which its critics have debated incessantly and singlemindedly. Some have explored its major medieval literary sources, influences, and parallels;[2] others have explored its direct and indirect religious, moral, or Christian aspects.[3] No one seems to have understood fully how the dual levels of the *Beowulf* article might apply to *The Lord of the Rings*, although Patricia Meyer Spacks suggests provocatively that at least one level does apply: Tolkien's view of the 'naked will and courage' of man necessary to combat chaos and death in the context of northern mythology (as opposed to Christianity) resembles the similar epic weapons of the hobbit-heroes of his trilogy.[4] In addition no critic has seemed to notice that even in genre and form this work combines an explicitly medieval bias (as epic, romance, or *chanson de geste*) with an implicitly Christian one (as fantasy or fairy-story).[5]

Its title, 'The Lord of the Rings', introduces the ambiguity of being a lord, a person with power over but also responsibility for others. Elsewhere in Tolkien's critical and creative works the lord has been depicted as an excessively proud Germanic earl bent on the sacrifice of his men for his own ends or as a humble Elf-king modelled on Christ, intent on sacrificing himself for the sake of his followers. So in this epic Sauron typifies the Germanic earl in his monstrous use of his slaves as Gandalf typifies the Elf-king or Christ-figure in his self-sacrifice during the battle with the Balrog. But there are hierarchies of both monstrous and heroic lords in this epic, whose plenitude has frustrated critical attempts to discern *the* hero as either Aragorn, Frodo, or Sam.[6] Aragorn may represent the Christian hero as Frodo and Sam represent the more Germanic hero of the subordinate warrior, yet all three remain epic heroes. The complexity of Tolkien's system of heroic and monstrous 'lords' in the trilogy becomes clearer through an examination of its structural unity.

In defining the parameters of the work's structure,[7] Tolkien declares that 'The only units of any structural significance are the books. These originally had each its title.'[8] Apparently he substituted titles for each of the three parts at the instigation of his publisher, although he preferred to regard it as a 'three-decker novel' instead of as a 'trilogy' in order to establish it as a single, unified work, not three separate works. Thus each of the three parts thematically and symbolically supports the crowning title, 'The Lord of the Rings', by revealing some aspect of the adversary or the hero through a related but subordinate title, and each part is itself supported thematically and symbolically by its two-book division. In *The Fellowship of the Ring* the focus falls upon the lord as both a hero and a monster, a divided self discussed above in Chapter One, 'The Critic as Monster'. Frodo as the 'lord' or keeper of the Ring in the first part mistakes the chief threat to the hobbit fellowship (a symbol of community) as physical and external (for example, the Black Riders) but matures enough to learn by the end of the second book that the chief threat exists in a more dangerous spiritual and internal form, whether within him as microcosm (the hero as monster) or within the Fellowship as macrocosm (his friend Boromir). *The Fellowship* as *Bildungsroman* echoes the development of the hero Bilbo in *The Hobbit* discussed in Chapter Two above, 'The King under the Mountain'. *The Two Towers* shifts attention from the divided self of the hero as monster to the more specifically Germanic but also Christian monster seen in Saruman (representing intellectual sin in Book Three) and Shelob (representing physical sin in Book Four) who occupy or guard the two towers of the title. This part duplicates material in *The Hobbit* outlining monstrosity in terms of the *Beowulf* article and the *Ancrene Wisse* discussed primarily in Chapter Two, 'The King under the Mountain'. The evil Germanic lord often has a good warrior to serve him; the figure of the good servant merges with the Christian king as healer (Aragorn) who dominates *The Return of the King* on opposition to the Germanic destroyer (Denethor) in Book Five, the consequences of whose reign lead to a 'Return' or regeneration in the macrocosm in Book Six. Ideas in this last part mirror Chapter Three's 'Christian King' appearing in fairy-stories and Chapter Four's 'Germanic King' appearing in medieval parodies. The structure of the epic then reveals a hierarchy of heroes and monsters implied by its title but also summoned from Tolkien's other critical and creative works.

I *The Fellowship of the Ring*: the Hero as Monster

Because it links the wandering Fellowship with the Ring, a subtitle for the first part of the epic might be 'All that is gold does not glitter, / Not all those who wander are lost.'9 The Ring appears valuable because it glitters; the wandering Fellowship appears lost. But in reality the gold ring may not be as simply valuable as it appears, and the Fellowship may not be lost; further, the person to whom the lines refer, despite his swart exterior and wandering behaviour as Strider the Ranger, may be real gold and definitely not lost. As the king of light opposed to the Dark Lord, he will return as king after the Ring has been finally returned to Mount Doom, ending the aspirations of the Lord of the Rings. 'The Fellowship of the Ring' as a title stresses the heroic mission of his 'followers' to advance the cause of the good king. The band of gold represents by synecdoche the power of the evil Lord of the Rings to be countered by the 'band' of the Fellowship, whether the four hobbits in Book One or the larger Fellowship of hobbits, wizard, elf, dwarf, and man in Book Two. Thematically, then, the title and its 'subtitle' suggest that appearance does not equal reality. Because the Fellowship is burdened with the responsibility of bearing the Ring and because its presence attracts evil, the greatest threat to the Fellowship and its mission comes not from without but within. The hero must realise that he can become a monster.

The two books of the *Fellowship* trace the process of this realisation: the first book centres on the presentation of evil as external and physical, requiring physical heroism to combat it, and the second book centres on the presentation of evil as internal and spiritual, requiring a spiritual heroism to combat it. The hero matures by coming to understand the character of good and evil – specifically, by descending into an underworld and then ascending into an overworld, a natural one in the first book and a supernatural one in the second. The second book then functions as a mirror image of the first. These two levels correspond to the two levels – Germanic and Christian – of *Beowulf* and *The Hobbit*. For Frodo, as for Beowulf and Bilbo, the ultimate enemy is himself.

Tolkien immediately defines 'the hero as monster' by introducing the divided self of Gollum-Smeagol and then, to ensure the reader's understanding of the hero as monster, Bilbo-as-Gollum. The Cain-like Smeagol rationalises the murder of his cousin Deagol for the gold ring he holds because it is his birthday (I, 84). He deserves a gift, something 'precious' like the Ring, because the occasion celebrates the fact of his birth, his special being. The parable of Smeagol's fall illustrates the nature of evil as *cupiditas* or avarice in the classical and literal sense. But as the root of all evil (in the words of Chaucer's Pardoner) *cupiditas* more generally and medievally represents that Augustinian selfishness usually personified as strong desire in the figure of Cupid. The two names of Gollum-Smeagol dramatise the fragmenting and divisive consequences of his fall into vice, the 'Gollum' the bestial sound of his swallowing as an expression of his gluttony and greed, the 'Smeagol' in its homonymic similarity to Deagol as a sound relating him to a group of others like him to establish his common hobbitness. For later his resemblance to the hobbits is revealed when good overpowers the evil in him and, as he witnesses his master Frodo asleep in Sam's lap, reaches out a hand to touch his knee in a caress. At that moment he seems 'an old weary hobbit, shrunken by the years that had carried him far beyond his time, beyond friends and kin, and the fields and streams of youth, an old starved pitiable thing' (II, 411). But also Tolkien takes care to present the good hobbit and heroic Bilbo as a divided self, 'stretched thin' into a Gollum-like being because of his years carrying the Ring. The scene opens after all with Bilbo's birthday party, to re-enact the original fall of Gollum. The role of Deagol is played by Bilbo's nephew Frodo: on Bilbo's birthday, instead of receiving a gift, Bilbo, like Gollum, must give away a gift – to the other hobbit relatives and friends, and to Frodo, recipient of the Ring. But at the moment of bequest Bilbo retreats into a Gollum-like personality illustrated by similar speech patterns: 'It is mine, I tell you. My own. My precious. Yes, my precious' (I, 59). Bilbo refuses to give away the Ring because he feels himself to be more deserving and Frodo less deserving of carrying it. Later the feeling is described as a realisation of the Other as monstrous (presumably with the concomitant belief in the self as good). In the parallel scene at the beginning of Book Two, Bilbo wishes to see the Ring so he reaches out a hand for Frodo to give it to him; Frodo reacts violently because 'a shadow seemed to have fallen between them, and through it he found himself eyeing a *little wrinkled creature with a hungry face and bony groping hands*. He felt a desire to strike him' (I, 306; my italics). The Ring then appropriately symbolises that wedding of self to self, of Gollum to Smeagol, in lieu of a wedding of self to Other.

The wedding of self to Other, as an expression of *caritas* hinted at in Gollum's momentary return to hobbitness when he almost loves his master Frodo, is symbolised by the 'band' of the Fellowship to which each member belongs. Such *caritas* opposes the view of the Other as monstrous. Even Frodo at first sees monstrous Gollum as despicable: 'What a pity that Bilbo did not stab that vile creature, when he had a chance!' (I, 92). But just as the hero can become monstrous so can the monster become heroic: it is Gollum who helps Frodo and Sam across the Dead Marshes and, more important, who inadvertently saves Frodo from himself and also saves Middle-earth by biting the Ring off Frodo's finger as they stand on the precipice of Mount Doom in the third part. So Gandalf cautions him to feel, not wrath or hatred, but love as pity: 'Pity? It was Pity that stayed his hand. Pity, and Mercy: not to strike without need.' (I, 92). Gandalf explains:

> Many that live deserve death. And some that die deserve life. Can you give it to them? Then do not be too eager to deal out death in judgment. For even the very wise cannot see all ends. I have not much hope that Gollum can be cured before he dies, but there is a chance of it. And he is bound up with the fate of the Ring. My heart tells me that he has some part to play yet, for good or ill, before the end; and when that comes, the pity of Bilbo may rule the fate of many – yours not least. (I, 93)

This pity as charity or love binding one man to another cements together the 'fellowship' of the hobbits and later the differing species; the 'chain' of love it creates contrasts with the chains of enslavement represented by Sauron's one Ring. Called a 'fair chain of love' in the Middle Ages, it supposedly bound one individual to another and as well bound together the macrocosm of the heavens: Boethius in *The Consolation of Philosophy* terms it a 'common bond of love by which all things seek to be held to the goal of good'.[10] After describing the love that 'binds together people joined by a sacred bond; love binds sacred marriages by chaste affections; love makes the laws which join true friends', Boethius wistfully declares, 'O how happy the human race would be, if that love which rules the heavens ruled also your souls!' (p. 41, Book Two, Poem 8). The chain of enslavement, in contrast, involves a hierarchy of power, beginning with the

> One Ring to rule them all, One Ring to find them,
> One Ring to bring them all and in the darkness bind them
> (I, vii),

and encompassing the seven dwarf-rings (could they be found) and the nine rings of the 'Mortal Men doomed to die', the Ringwraiths. If love binds together the heavens and the hierarchy of species known as the Great Chain of Being in the Middle Ages, which included angels, man, beasts, birds, fish, plants, and stones, then hate and envy, pride and avarice bind together the hierarchy of species under the aegis of the One Ring of Sauron the fallen Vala. Only the 'Three Rings for the Elven-kings under the sky' – the loftiest and most noble species – were never made by Sauron because, says Elrond, the elves 'did not desire strength or domination or hoarded wealth, but understanding, making, and healing, to preserve all things unstained' (I, 352). Tolkien intentionally contrasts the hierarchy of good characters linked by the symbolic value of fellowship into an invisible band or chain of love with the hierarchy of evil characters and fallen characters linked by the literal rings of enslavement – a chain of sin.[11] It is for this reason that the miniature Fellowship of hobbits in the first book draws together in love different representatives from hobbit 'species' or families – Baggins, Took, Brandybuck, Gamgee – as the larger Fellowship in the second book draws together representatives from different species – the four hobbit representatives, Gimli the dwarf, Strider and Boromir the men, Legolas the elf, and Gandalf the wizard. In both cases, however, these representatives are all young – the heirs of the equivalents of the 'old men' who must revitalise and renew Middle-earth because it too has become 'old' and decrepit, governed by the spiritually old and corrupt influence of Sauron. Symbolically, then, these 'heirs' as young men represent vitality, life, newness: Frodo is Bilbo's nephew and heir, Gimli is Gloin's, Legolas is Thranduil's, Strider is Isildur's, Boromir is Denethor's, and the remaining hobbits are the still youthful children of their aged fathers. Only Gandalf as the good counterpart to Sauron is 'old'. In part he constitutes a spiritual guide for Frodo, especially in Book Two, as Aragorn-Strider constitutes a physical one in Book One.

The necessity for the young figure to become the saviour hero (like the *novus homo*) of the old is introduced by Tolkien in the first pages of *The Fellowship*. Note the spiritual oldness of the hobbit 'fathers' of the miniature Fellowship who view the different or queer as alien, evil, monstrous, dangerous: they lack charity, pity, understanding. They condemn the Brandybucks of Buckland as a 'queer breed' for engaging in unnatural (for hobbits at least) activities on water (I, 45). Yet these old hobbits are not evil, merely 'old'. Even the Gaffer vindicates Bag End and its 'queer folk' by admitting: 'There's some not far away that wouldn't offer a pint of beer to a friend, if they lived in a hole with golden walls. But they do things proper at Bag End' (I, 47). His oldness is characteristic of the Old Law of Justice ('proper') rather than the New Law of Mercy. They also lack imagination, an awareness of the spirit rather than the letter. Sam's father expresses a literalism and earthiness similar to Sauron's: *'Elves and Dragons!* I says to him. *Cabbages and potatoes are better for me and you'* (I, 47). This 'Old Man' Tolkien casts in the role as the Old Adam for whom Christ as the New Adam will function as a replacement and redeemer: a gardener like Adam at Bag End, he condemns that of which he cannot conceive for that of which he can, cabbages and potatoes, and presents his condemnation in the appropriately-named inn of the 'Ivy Bush'. His son Sam in effect will become the New Adam of the Shire by the trilogy's end. Generally, however, earth-bound hobbits (inhabiting holes under ground) display a similar lack of imagination symbolised by their delight in the pyrotechnic dragon created by Gandalf – they may not be able to imagine elves and dragons but they love what they can *see*, a 'terribly life-like' dragon leaving nothing to the imagination (I, 52). This dragon, however, poses no threat to their lives – in fact, it represents the 'signal for supper'.

The 'new man' represented by the hobbits Frodo, Sam, Merry, and Pippin then must overcome a natural inclination toward 'oldness', toward the life of the senses inherent in the hobbit love of food, comfort, warm shelter, entertainment, good tobacco. All of them do so by the trilogy's end, but only Frodo as Ring-bearer actually changes dramatically and centrally by the end of *The Fellowship*. His education, both verbal and experiential, begins with the gift of the Ring after Bilbo's Birthday Party.

Designated as Bilbo's heir and recipient of the Ring in the Birthday Party (Chapters 1–5) in the first book he is also designated as the official Ring-bearer after the Council of Elrond (Chapters 1–3) in the second book, to which it is parallel. In the first book Gandalf relates the history of Gollum's discovery of the Ring and Bilbo's winning of it, and he explains its nature and properties; in the second book at this similar gathering the history of the Ring from its creation by Sauron to the present and the roles therein of various species is related. The birthday party that allows Bilbo to 'disappear' as if by magic from the Shire is like the Council that allows Frodo and other members of the Fellowship to 'disappear' as if by magic from Middle-earth – and the searching Eye of Sauron, for he will never imagine them carrying the Ring *back* to Mordor. Further, the distribution of gifts to friends and relatives after the party resembles the Council's decision to give back the 'gift' of the Ring to its 'relative', the mother lode of Mount Doom. The gifts in each episode make explicit the flaws of the recipient: Adelard Took, for example, receives an umbrella because he has stolen so many from Bilbo. In a sense Sauron too will indirectly receive exactly what he has always wanted and. has continually tried to usurp or steal – the Ring. The point of these parallels should be clear: the concept of the divided self or the hero as monster was revealed in the symbolic Birthday Party through the figures of Gollum-Smeagol, Bilbo-Gollum, Frodo-Gollum – the hero as monster suggested by the notion of the 'birthday'. For the reader, Tolkien warns that the most dangerous evil really springs from inside, not from outside. This message introduced at the beginning of the volume is what Frodo must learn by its end. The 'Council of Elrond', its very title suggesting egalitarian debate among members of a community rather than group celebration of an individual, symbolically poses the converse message that the most beneficial good similarly springs from the inside but must be directed toward the community rather than oneself. The humblest member of the Council – the insignificant hobbit Frodo – is ultimately chosen to pursue the mission of the Ring because he *is* insignificant. His insignificance in the community there contrasts with Bilbo's significance as a member of the Shire community. However, as 'The Birthday Party' indicated the presence of evil among relatives (the greedy and self-aggrandising Sackville-Bagginses) so The 'Council of Elrond' indicates the potential of evil threatening the Fellowship from within through the greed and self-aggrandisement of some of its members – men.

In the first book Frodo comes to understand evil as external and physical through the descent into the Old Forest, a parallel underworld to the supernatural underworld of Moria in the second book.[12] Old Man Willow and the barrow-wights both represent the natural process of death caused, in Christian terms, by the Fall of man. Originally the Old Forest consisted of the 'fathers of the fathers of trees' whose 'countless years had filled them with pride and rooted wisdom, and with malice' (I, 181), as if they had sprung from the one Tree of Knowledge of Good and Evil in Eden. The ensuing history of human civilisation after the Fall of Adam and Eve resulted in similar falls and deaths: 'There was victory and defeat; and towers fell, fortresses were burned, and flames went up into the sky. Gold was piled on the biers of dead kings and queens; and mounds covered them and the stone doors were shut; and the grass grew over all' (I, 181). As Old Man Willow and his malice represents the living embodiment of the parent Tree of Death, so the barrow-wights represent the ghostly embodiment of the dead parent civilisations of men: 'Barrow-wights walked in the hollow places with a clink of rings on cold fingers, and gold chains in the wind' (I, 181). The hobbits' first clue to the character of the *Old* Forest (note again Tolkien's emphasis on oldness) resides in the falling of the hobbits' spirits – a 'dying' of merriment – when they first enter. Their fear, depression, and gloom are followed by the deathlike sleep (again, a result of the Fall) as the chief weapon of Old Man Willow (I, 165). All growth in Nature is abetted by sleep and ends in death, usually after oldness (again, the Old Man Willow figure). The barrow-wights who attack the hobbits later in the Old Forest are also linked to the earth like the roots of Old Man Willow but here through the barrow, a man-made grave which they inhabit as ghosts. The song of the barrow-wights invokes coldness and death, and specifically the 'bed' of the human grave:

> Cold be hand and heart and bone,
> and cold be sleep under stone:
> never more to wake on stony bed,
> never, till the Sun fails and the Moon is dead.
> In the black wind the stars shall die,
> and still on gold here let them lie.
>
> (I, 195)

The attacks of the Old Man Willow and the barrow-wights on the hobbits are stopped by Tom Bombadil who, along with his mate Goldberry, personify their complementary and positive counter-parts in Nature. The principle of growth and revivification of all living things balances the process of mutability and death: what Goldberry lauds as 'spring-time and summer-time, and spring again after!' (I, 173), omitting autumn and winter as antithetical seasons. Tom Bombadil as master of trees, grasses, and the living things of the land (I, 174) complements the 'fair river-daughter' dressed in a gown 'green as young reeds, shot with silver like beads of dew', her feet surrounded by water-lilies (I, 172). Because their role in Nature involves the maintenance of the existing order, their songs often praise the Middle-earth equivalent of the medieval Chain of Being:

> Let us sing together
> Of sun, stars, moon and mist, rain and cloudy weather,
> Light on the budding leaf, dew on the feather,
> Wind on the open hill, bells on the heather,
> Reeds by the shady pool, lilies on the water:
> Old Tom Bombadil and the River-daughter!
>
> (I, 171)

As the Old Forest depresses the hobbits, Tom Bombadil cheers them up so much that, by the time they reach his house, 'half their weariness and all their fears had fallen from them' (I, 171). It is no accident that Tom Bombadil always seems to be laughing and singing joyously.

Frodo learns from the descent into this underworld of the Old Forest that the presence of mutability, change, and death in the world is natural and continually repaired by growth and new life. In the second book he learns through a parallel descent into the Mines of Moria that the spiritual form of death represented by sin stems from within the individual but is redeemed by the 'new life' of wisdom and virtue counselled by Galadriel, the supernatural equivalent of Tom Bombadil who resides in the paradisal Lothlórien. The descent also involves a return to the tragic past of the dwarves, who fell because of the 'oldness' of their kings, their avarice; the ascent involves an encounter with the eternal present of Lothlórien, where all remains new and young, and filled with the healing spirit of elven mercy and *caritas*.

The dwarves led by both Durin and later Balin fell because of their greed for the jewels mined in Moria – its depths a metaphorical equivalent of Old Man Willow's buried roots and the deep barrows inhabited by the wights. But unlike the death pervading the Old Forest, the death represented by the Mines is voluntary, because spiritual: it exists in the form of avarice. Gandalf declares that 'even as *mithril* was the foundation of their wealth, so also it was their destruction: they delved too greedily and too deep, and disturbed that from which they fled, Durin's Bane' (I, 413). Durin's Bane, the Balrog, monstrously projects their internal vice, which resurfaces later to down other dwarves including Balin. It is no accident that Balin dies at Mirrormere, a very dark mirror in which he is blind to himself. His mistaken goal of *mithril* and jewels contrasts with that of the elves of Lórien, whose Galadriel possesses a clear mirror of wisdom.

Lórien of the Blossom boasts an Eternal Spring where 'ever bloom the winter flowers in the unfading grass' (I, 454), a 'vanished world' where the shapes and colours are pristine and new, for 'No blemish or sickness or deformity could be seen in anything that grew upon the earth. On the land of Lórien there was no stain' (I, 454–5). In this paradise of restoration, like that of Niggle in 'Leaf by Niggle', time almost ceases to pass and seems even to reverse so that 'the grim years were removed from the face of Aragorn, and he seemed clothed in white, a young lord tall and fair' (I, 456). Evil does not exist in this land or in Galadriel unless brought in from the outside (I, 464). The physical and spiritual regeneration or 'life' characteristic of these elves is embodied in their lembas, a food that restores spirits and lasts exceedingly long – a type of communion offered to the weary travellers. Other gifts of the Lady Galadriel – the rope, magic cloaks, golden hairs, phial of light, seeds of elanor – later aid them either physically or spiritually at times of crisis in their quest almost as Christian grace in material form. Like Adam and Eve forced to leave Paradise for the wilderness, although taking with them its memory as a 'paradise within, happier far', in Miltonic terms, the travellers leave Lórien knowing 'the danger of light and joy' (I, 490). Legolas reminds Gimli the dwarf that 'the least reward that you shall have is that the memory of Lothlórien shall remain ever clear and unstained in your heart, and shall neither fade nor grow stale' (I, 490). Gimli's dwarfish and earth-bound nature compels him to deny the therapeutic value of memory: 'Memory is not what the heart desires. That is only a mirror, be it clear as Kheled-zâram' (I, 490). The mirror to which he refers in Westron is called 'Mirrormere' and, instead of reflecting back the faces of gazers, portrays only the reflection of a crown of stars representing Durin's own desire. In contrast is the Mirror of Galadriel with its vision of the Eternal Present connoting supernatural wisdom, for it invites the gazer to 'see' or understand himself, however unpleasant. Gimli is wrong, memory *is* a mirror and reflects back the consolation of truth, at least for elves, whose 'memory is more like to the waking world than to a dream. Not so for Dwarves' (I, 490).

This lesson in natural and supernatural evil and good also functions as a mirror for Frodo to see himself. He must learn there is both dwarf and elf in his heart, a Mines of Moria and Lothlórien buried in his psyche. Having learned, he must then exercise free will in choosing either good or evil, usually experienced in terms of putting on or taking off the Ring at times of external or internal danger. While his initial exercises are fraught with mistakes in judgement, the inability to distinguish impulse from deliberation or an external summons from an internal decision, eventually he does learn to control his own desires and resist the will of others. Told by Gandalf to fling the Ring into the fire after just receiving it, 'with an effort of will he made a movement, as if to cast it away – but he found that he had put it back in his pocket' (I, 94). As he practises he grows more adept but still slips – as when at the Inn of the Prancing Pony his singing and dancing attempt to divert the attention of Pippin's audience from the tale of Bilbo's birthday party allows him to become so 'pleased with himself' that he puts on the Ring by mistake and becomes embarrassingly invisible. The physical dangers he faces in these encounters culminate in the attack of the Black Riders one night and later at the Ford. The Ring in the first instance so controls his will that 'his terror was swallowed up in a sudden temptation to put on the Ring. The desire to do this laid hold of him, and he could think of nothing else . . . at last he slowly drew out the chain, and slipped the Ring on the forefinger of his left hand' (I, 262–3). As a consequence he can see the Ringwraiths as they really are but unfortunately so can they see him, enough to wound him in the shoulder. The worst test in the first book involves the encounter at the Ford. Counselled first by Gandalf to 'Ride' from the Black Rider attacking them, he is counselled silently by the Riders to wait. When his strength to refuse diminishes he is saved first by Glorfindel, who addresses his horse in Elvish to flee, and again by Gandalf, who drowns the horses of the Black Riders when they prevent Frodo's horse from crossing the Ford. While he fails these major tests in the first book and must rely on *dei ex machina* to save himself, his newly-established valour and courage represent the first steps toward attaining the higher form of heroism expressed by wisdom and self-control in the second book.

The physical heroism of Frodo combats physical dangers in Book One – his cry for help when Merry is caught by Old Man Willow, his stabbing of the barrow-wight's hand as it approaches the bound Sam, his dancing and singing to protect Pippin and their mission from discovery, his stabbing of the foot of one Rider during the night-attack, and his valour (brandishing his sword) and courage (refusing to put on the Ring, telling the Riders to return to Mordor) at the edge of the Ford. But this last incident reveals his spiritual naïveté: he believes physical gestures of heroism will ward off the Black Riders. Only after his education in the second book, which details supernatural death and regeneration instead of its more natural and physical forms as in the first book, does he begin to understand the necessity of *sapientia* in addition to that heroism expressed by the concept of *fortitudo*. In the last chapter, 'The Breaking of the Fellowship', he faces a threat from the proud and avaricious Boromir *within* the macrocosm of the Fellowship. Fleeing from him he puts on the Ring to render himself invisible and safe. But this unwise move allows him to see, as he sits, symbolically, upon Amon Hen, or the Hill of the Eye of the Men of Numenor, Sauron's own searching Eye. What results is a second internal danger – the threat from within Frodo the microcosm. A battle is staged within his psyche , and he is pulled first one way, then another, until Frodo, as a fully developed moral hero, exercises the faculty of free will with complete self-control:

> He heard himself crying out: *Never, never!* Or was it: *Verily I come, I come to you?* He could not tell. Then as a flash from some other point of power there came to his mind another thought: *Take it off! Take it off! Fool, take it off! Take off the Ring!*
> The two powers strove in him. For a moment, perfectly balanced between their piercing points, he writhed, tormented. Suddenly he was aware of himself again. Frodo, neither the Voice nor the Eye: free to choose, and with one remaining instant in which to do so. He took the Ring off his finger. (I, 519)

In this incident parallel to the encounter of the Riders at the Ford in the last chapter of the first book Frodo here rescues *himself* instead of being rescued by Glorfindel or Gandalf. Further, in proving his moral education by the realisation he must wage his own quest alone to protect both their mission and the other members of the Fellowship, he displays *fortitudo et sapientia* and *caritas* – hence he acts as that saviour of the Fellowship earlier witnessed in the figures of Tom Bombadil and Strider in the first book and Gandalf and Galadriel in the second. His education complete, Frodo can now function as a hero for he understands he may, at any time, become a monster.

The turning point in the narrative allows a shift in Tolkien's theme and the beginning of the second part of the epic novel in *The Two Towers*. The remaining members of the Fellowship are divided into two separate groups in this next book, division symbolising thematically not only the nature of conflict in battle in the macrocosm but also the psychic fragmentation resulting from evil. It is no mistake that the title is 'The *Two* Towers' – the double, again, symptomatic of the divided self. There are not only two towers but two monsters.

II *The Two Towers*: the Germanic King

The two towers of the title belong to Saruman and in a sense to Shelob because the quest of the remainder of the Fellowship in Book Three culminates in an attack on Orthanc and the quest of Frodo and Sam in Book Four leads to their 'attack' on Cirith Ungol, the sentry tower at the border of Mordor guarded by the giant spider. Both Orthanc and Cirith Ungol copy the greatest tower of all, the Dark Tower of Sauron described as a 'fortress, armoury, prison, furnace . . . secure in its pride and its immeasurable strength' (II, 204). This second part of *The Lord of the Rings* through these two monsters represented by their towers defines the nature of the evil monster in greater detail than in the first part. Thus it introduces the notion of the Christian deadly sins embodied in the monsters, which must be combated by very Germanic heroes.

The tower image is informed by the Tower of Babel in Genesis 11. In this biblical passage at first 'Throughout the earth men spoke the same language, with the same vocabulary', but then the sons of Noah built a town and 'a tower with its top reaching heaven'. They decided, 'Let us make a name for ourselves, so that we may not be scattered about the whole earth'.[13] Their desire to reach heaven and 'make a name' for themselves represents the same desire of Adam and Eve for godhead. Because they believe 'There will be nothing too hard for them to do' (11:6–7), the Lord frustrates their desire by 'confusing' their language and scattering them over the earth.

The selfishness, or *cupiditas*, symbolised by the Tower of Babel shows how a preoccupation with self at the expense of the Other or of God can lead to confusion, alienation, division. The Two Towers in Tolkien's work further break down this idea of *cupiditas* as perversion of self. The Tower of Saruman, or Orthanc, means 'Mount Fang' in Elvish but 'Cunning Mind' in the language of the Mark to suggest perversion of the mind; the Tower of Shelob, or Cirith Ungol, means 'Pass of the Spider' to suggest perversion of the body. While the creation of the Tower of Babel results in differing languages to divide the peoples, the two towers in Tolkien express division in a more microcosmic sense, in terms of the separation and perversion of the two parts of the self. Saruman's intellectual perversion has shaped his tower (formerly inhabited by the wardens of Gondor) to 'his shifting purposes, and made it better, as he thought, being deceived – for all those arts and subtle devices, for which he forsook his former wisdom, and which fondly he imagined were his own, came but from Mordor' (II, 204). Specifically his pride and envy of Sauron impel him to achieve ever more power as his avarice impels him to seek the Ring and conquer more lands and forests through wrathful wars. Like Saruman, Shelob 'served none but herself' but in a very different, more bestial way by 'drinking the blood of Elves and Men, bloated and grown fat with endless brooding on her feasts, weaving webs of shadow; for all living things were her food, and her vomit darkness' (II, 422). Her gluttony is revealed in her insatiable appetite, her sloth in her demands that others bring her food, her lechery in her many bastards (perhaps appropriately and symbolically quelled by Sam's penetration of her belly with his sword). Never can she achieve the higher forms of perversion manifested by Saruman: 'Little she knew of or cared for towers, or rings, or anything devised by mind or hand, who only desired death for all others, mind and body, and for herself a glut of life, alone, swollen till the mountains could no longer hold her up' (II, 423). Guarding the gateway to Mordor at Cirith Ungol she suggests another guardian – of the gateway to Hell. In *Paradise Lost* Satan's daughter Sin mated with her father to beget Death, the latter of whom pursued her lecherous charms relentlessly and incessantly. In this case Shelob is depicted not as Satan's daughter but as Sauron's cat (II, 424).

Tolkien shows the analogy between the two monsters and their towers by structuring their books similarly. The perversion of mind embodied in Saruman is expressed by the difficulty in communication through or understanding of words or gestures in Book Three and the perversion of body personified in Shelob is expressed by the difficulty in finding food and shelter, hospitality, in Book Four. Specifically Wormtongue, Grishnákh, and Saruman all display aspects of the higher sins of pride, avarice, envy, and wrath through their incomprehension or manipulation of language. Gollum and Shelob both illustrate the lower sins of gluttony, sloth, and lechery. Each book centres on the adventures of only part of the Fellowship, the nobler members in Book Three (Legolas, Gimli, Aragorn, and Merry and Pippin) and the more humble members in Book Four (Sam and Frodo). In each book too the adventures progressively become more dangerous, the enemies encountered more vicious.

The Uruk-hai in Book Three illustrate the disorder and contention caused by the literal failure to understand languages. When Pippin first awakens after being captured, he can understand only some of the orcs' language: 'Apparently the members of two or three quite different tribes were present, and they could not understand one another's orc-speech. There was an angry debate concerning what they were to do now: which way they were to take and what should be done with the prisoners' (II, 60). The debate advances to quarrel and then to murder when Saruman's Uglúk of the Uruk-hai kills two of Sauron's orcs led by Grishnákh. The parable suggests that the tongues of different species or peoples create misunderstanding and hence conflict, disorder, death, because of the inability to transcend selfish interests. Because they do not adhere to a common purpose their enmity allows the hobbits their freedom when Grishnákh's desire for the Ring overcomes his judgement and he unties the hobbits just before his death.

This literal failure to communicate is followed in Book Three by a description of a deliberate manipulation of language so that misunderstanding will occur. Worm*tongue*'s ill-counsel renders the king impotent and his people leaderless. As a good counsellor Gandalf begs Theoden to 'come out before your doors and look abroad. Too long have you sat in shadows and trusted to twisted tales and crooked promptings' (II, 151). When Theoden spurns the 'forked tongue' of the 'witless worm' (the Satanic parallels are intentional) in exchange for wise counsel he leaves the darkness, stands erect, and drops his staff to act as 'one new-awakened'. Without manipulating a belittling language into death and despair-dealing weapons, like Wormtongue, Gandalf wisely counsels life and hope. Such good words unite the Rohirrim and the Fellowship in a common purpose – fighting Saruman – rather than one which divides, like that of the quarrelsome Uruk-hair and orcs.

If Gandalf awakens Theoden from a sleep caused by evil counsel, Merry and Pippin awaken Treebeard from no counsel at all, he has so sleepily neglected his charge as Shepherd of the Trees. While Treebeard has been used as a source of information by Saruman, the latter has not reciprocated, even evilly: 'his face, as I remember it . . . became like windows in a stone wall: windows with shutters inside' (II, 96). But Treebeard must realise the threat to Fangorn posed by Saruman, who 'has a mind of metal and wheels; and he does not care for growing things, except as far as they serve him for the moment' (II, 96). He has abused Nature's growing things by destroying the trees and twisted human nature by creating mutants and enslaving the will of men like Theoden to obtain his will. In the Entmoot, an orderly civilised debate in contrast to the quarrels of the orcs and the one-sided insinuations of Wormtongue, language serves properly to unite the ents by awakening them to Saruman's threat. These talking trees – signify-

ing the principle of reason and order inherent in Nature as the
higher complement to the principle of life and growth signified by
Tom Bombadil – join with the men of Rohan (as Riders complementary to the Rangers we met in the figure of Strider in the
first book) to combat the evil represented by 'Cunning Mind'.

These episodes delineating the problem of language and communication as an attempt to join with or separate from the Other
culminate in the most important one in the chapter entitled 'The
Voice of Saruman', in which, in the final debate between the fallen
and the reborn wizards, Saruman fails to use language cunningly
enough to obtain his end and hence he loses, literally and
symbolically, that chief weapon of the 'cunning mind', the *palantir*
('far-seer'). Unctuous Saruman almost convinces the group that he
is a gentle man much put upon who only desires to meet the
mighty Theoden. But Gimli wisely perceives that 'The words of
this wizard stand on their heads. . . . In the language of Orthanc
help means ruin, and saving means slaying, that is plain' (II, 235).
In addition, Eomer and Theoden resist the temptation to believe the
wily ex-wizard, so that his truly corrupt nature is then revealed
through the demeaning imprecations he directs toward the house
of Eorl.

The emphasis upon language in this book shows that human
speech can reflect man's highest and lowest aspirations: good
words can express the love for another as cunning words can seek
to subvert another for the speaker's own selfish ends. The
archetypal Word is Christ as the Incarnation of God's love; but
words or speech in general, according to St Thomas Aquinas in his
essay 'On Kingship', naturally distinguishes man from the beast
because it expresses his rational nature. However, the misuse of
man's reason to acquire knowledge forbidden him by God leads to
his spiritual degeneration and the dehumanisation of other men.
On the one hand such behaviour marks Saruman as a perverted
wizard accompanied by his equally perverted servant Wormtongue – their perversion makes them monstrous. On the other
hand this book is filled with examples of the heroes' difficulty in
communicating with others and understanding the signs and
signals of another's language, to underscore the extent of Saruman's perversion.

Thus, for example, when Aragorn, Legolas, and Gimli find the
hobbits missing but their whereabouts unknown they face an 'evil
choice' because of this lack of communication, just as Merry and

Pippin, once captured, almost succumb to despair because they do
not know where they are or where they are going (II, 59). In their
attempt to pursue the hobbits, the remainder of the Fellowship
must learn to 'read' a puzzling sign-language: the letter S em-
blazoned on a dead orc's shield (killed in Boromir's defence of the
hobbits), the footprints of Sam leading *into* the water but not back
again (II, 25), the heap of dead orcs without any clue to the hobbits'
presence (II, 53), the appearance of a strange old man bearing away
their horses (II, 116), the mystery of the bound hobbits' apparent
escape (II, 116). All of these signs or riddles can be explained, and
indeed, as Aragorn suggests, 'we must guess the riddles, if we are
to choose our course rightly' (II, 21). Man's quest symbolically
depends on his correct use of his reason; the temptation is to know
more than one should by consulting a magical device like the
palantir.

If Book Three demonstrates the intellectual nature of sin then
Book Four demonstrates its physical nature. Although the structure of Shelob's tower of Cirith Ungol ends this book as Orthanc
ends the Third, it is never described in this part. Instead another
tower – Minas Morgul – introduces the weary group to the land
they approach at the book's end. In appearance it resembles a
human corpse:

> Paler indeed than the moon ailing in some slow eclipse was the
> light of it now, wavering and blowing like a noisome exhalation
> of decay, a *corpse-light*, a light that illuminated nothing. In the
> walls and tower windows showed, like countless black holes
> *looking inward* into emptiness; but the topmost course of the
> tower revolved slowly, first one way and then another, *a huge
> ghostly head* leering into the night. (II, 396–7, my italics)

The holes might be a skull's. As a type of corpse it focuses attention
on the human body, whose perverse desires preoccupy Tolkien in
this book.

So Gollum's obsession with fish and dark things of the earth
disgusts Frodo and Sam: his name as the sound of swallowing
aptly characterises his monstrously gluttonous nature. Again,
when he guides them across the Dead Marshes it is dead bodies
from the battle between Sauron and the Alliance in the Third Age,
or their appearance, which float beneath the surface and tempt
Gollum's appetite (II, 297). But the hobbits' appetites result in

trouble too: they are captured by Faramir when the smoke of the fire for the rabbit stew cooked by Sam and generously intended for Frodo is detected (just as Gollum is captured by Frodo at Faramir's when he hunts fish in the Forbidden Pool). Faramir's chief gift to the weary hobbits is a most welcome hospitality, including food and shelter as a respite from the barren wasteland they traverse. Finally, the hobbits are themselves intended as food by Gollum for the insatiable spider Shelob. Truly the monster (whether Gollum or Shelob) is depicted as a glutton just as the hero, past, present, or future (the corpse, the hobbits, Faramir), is depicted as food or life throughout this book. Physical life can end without food to sustain the body; it can also end, as the previous book indicated, because of an inaccurate interpretation of language to guide rational judgement.

These monsters representing sin are opposed by heroes represented as Germanic kings and warriors. As we have seen, Theoden the weak leader of Rohan is transformed by Gandalf's encouragement into a very heroic Germanic king in Book Three, unlike the proud Beorhtnoth of 'The Battle of Maldon'. In Book Four the Germanic warrior or subordinate (chiefly Sam) vows to lend his aid to his master out of love and loyalty like the old retainer Beorhtwold in 'The Battle of Maldon'. The bond between the king as head of a nation and the reason as 'lord' of the individual corresponds to that between the subordinate warrior as servant of the king and the subordinate body.

To enhance these Germanic correspondences Tolkien describes Rohan as an Old English nation complete with appropriate names[14] and includes a suspicious hall-guardian named Hama very similar to one in *Beowulf* and an *ubi sunt* poem modelled on a passage from the Old English 'Wanderer':

Where now the horse and rider? Where is the horn that was blowing?
Where is the helm and the hauberk, and the bright hair flowing?
(II, 142)

Where went the horse, where went the man? Where went the treasure-giver?

Where went the seats of banquets? Where are the hall-joys?[15]

In addition throughout Book Three Tolkien stresses the physical heroism of the Rohirrim and the Fellowship in the battle at Helm's Deep, which resembles those described in 'The Battle of Maldon', 'Brunnanburh', and 'The Fight at Finnsburg'. But in Book Four the heroism of the 'warrior' depends more on love and loyalty than on expressions of valour in battle.

Four major subordinates emerge, Gollum, Sam, Frodo, and Faramir. Each offers a very Germanic oath of allegiance to his master or lord: Gollum in pledging not to run away if he is untied swears by the Ring that 'I will serve the master of the Precious' (II, 285). So Frodo becomes a lord, 'a tall stern shadow, a mighty lord who hid his brightness in grey cloud, and at his feet a whining dog' (II, 285). Gollum must also swear an oath to Faramir never to return to the Forbidden Pool or lead others there (II, 379). Sam similarly serves his master Frodo but like Gollum betrays him, not to Shelob but to Faramir, by cooking the rabbit stew. Likewise Frodo the master seems to betray his servant Gollum by capturing him at the Forbidden Pool even though he has actually saved him from death at the hands of Faramir's men, because 'The servant has a claim on the master for service, even service in fear' (II, 375). Finally, because Faramir has granted Frodo his protection Frodo offers him his service, while simultaneously requesting a similar protection for Frodo's servant Gollum: 'take this creature, this Smeagol, under your protection' (II, 380). Ultimately even Faramir has vowed to serve his father and lord, Denethor, by protecting this isolated post. In the next part of the epic Denethor will view Faramir's service as incomplete, a betrayal. Because he has not died instead of his brother Boromir, he will seem to fail just as the warriors lying in the Dead Marshes have apparently succeeded only too well, given the fact of their death in battle. While the exchange of valour or service for protection by a lord duplicates the Germanic contract between warrior and king, the exchange in *The Two Towers* seems fraught with difficulty either because of the apparent laxity of the lord or the apparent disloyalty of the subordinate.

The enemy, interestingly enough, functions primarily as a symbolic perversion of Christian rather than Germanic values, but still there is some correspondence between the *ofermod* of the Germanic king and the *superbia* of the Christian, both leading to other, lesser sins. The Germanic emphasis in this volume does continue in the next part of the epic, but ultimately merges with a more Christian definition of both servant and king.

III *The Return of The King*: the **Christian King**

This part of *The Lord of the Rings* sees the climax of the struggle between good and evil through battle between the Satanlike Dark Lord and the Christlike true king, Aragorn. Because he 'returns' to his people to accept the mantle of responsibility the volume is entitled 'The Return of the King', with emphasis upon kingship in Book Five and return in Book Six. Dramatic foils for the Christian king as the good steward are provided in Book Five by the good and bad Germanic lords Theoden and Denethor, whose names suggest anagrams of each other. The good Germanic subordinates Pippin and Merry, whose notion of service echoes that of the good Christian, similarly act as foils for the archetypal Christian servant Sam, whose exemplary love for his master Frodo transcends all normal bounds in Book Six. Finally, the concept of renewal attendant upon the return of the king pervades the latter part of the sixth book as a fitting coda to the story of the triumph of the true king over the false one.

The contrast between the two Germanic lords is highlighted early in Book Five by the offers of service presented respectively by Pippin to Denethor in Chapter One and by Merry to Theoden in Chapter Two. As the Old Man, the Germanic king more interested in glory and honour than in his men's welfare, Denethor belittles Pippin because he assumes smallness of size equals smallness of service. This literalistic mistake has been made earlier by other 'Old Men', especially *Beowulf* critics, the narrator of *The Hobbit*, and Nokes in 'Smith of Wootton Major'. Why, Denethor muses, did the 'halfling' escape the orcs when his much larger son Boromir did not? In return for Denethor's loss Pippin feels moved – by pride – to offer in exchange himself, but as an eye-for-an-eye, justly-rendered payment of a debt: 'Then Pippin looked the old man in the eye, for pride stirred strangely within him, still stung by the scorn and suspicion in that cold voice. "Little service, no doubt, will so great a lord of Men think to find in a hobbit, a halfling from the northern Shire; yet such as it is, I will offer it, in payment of my debt" ' (III, 30). His offer is legalised by a contractual vow binding him both to Gondor and the Steward of the realm either until death takes him or his lord releases him. The specific details of the contract invoke the usual terms of the bond between lord and warrior according to the Germanic *comitatus* ethic: he must not 'fail to reward that which is given: fealty with love, valour with honour, oath-breaking with vengeance' (III, 31).

Merry's vow to Theoden, in contrast, expresses a voluntary love for, rather than involuntary duty to, his king characteristic of the ideal Germanic subordinate in Tolkien's 'Ofermod' commentary. And Theoden, unlike Denethor, represents the ideal Germanic lord who truly loves instead of uses his men. Viewing Merry as an equal he invites him to eat, drink, talk, and ride with him, later suggesting that as his esquire he ride on a hill-pony especially found for him. Merry responds to this loving gesture with one equally loving and spontaneous. 'Filled suddenly with love for this old man, he knelt on one knee, and took his hand and kissed it. "May I lay the sword of Meriadoc of the Shire on your lap, Théoden King?" he cried. "Receive my service, if you will!" ' (III, 59). In lieu of the legal contract of the lord Denethor and the servant Pippin there is a verbal promise of familial love: ' "As a father you shall be to me," said Merry' (III, 59).

These private vows of individual service to the governors of Gondor and Rohan are followed in Chapters Two and Three by more public demonstrations of national or racial service. In the first incident the previous Oathbreakers of the past – the Dead of the Grey Company – redeem their past negligence by bringing aid to Aragorn in response to his summons. This contractual obligation fulfilled according to the letter of prophecy, Theoden and his Rohirrim can fulfil their enthusiastic and loving pledge of aid by journeying to Gondor. They themselves are accompanied by the Wild Men in Chapter Five as a symbolic corollary to their spontaneity, love, and enthusiasm – the new law of the spirit.

In addition two oathmakers of Rohan literally violate their private vows of individual service but actually render far greater service than any outlined in a verbal contract. When Eowyn relinquishes her duty to Theoden of taking charge of the people until his return by disguising herself as Dernhelm so that she may fight in battle, she also allows Merry to relinquish his vow to Theoden when he secretly rides behind her into battle. But when Theoden is felled by the Nazgûl Lord it is she who avenges him – Dernhelm 'wept, for he had loved his lord as a father' (III, 141) – as well as Merry – "King's man? King's man!" his heart cried within him. "You must stay by him. As a father you shall be to me, you said" ' (III, 141). Dernhelm slays the winged creature ridden by the Lord of the Nazgûl; Merry helps her slay the Lord. The service they render, a vengeance impelled by pity and love for their lord, is directed not only to the dead king and father Theoden, or to Rohan and Gondor, but to all of Middle-earth. Interestingly, her bravery in battle arouses Merry's: 'Pity filled his heart and great wonder, and suddenly the slow-kindled courage of his race awoke. He clenched his hand. She should not die, so fair, so desperate! At least she should not die alone, unaided' (III, 142). Simple love for another results in Merry's most charitable and heroic act. These subordinates have completely fulfilled the spirit, if not the letter, of their pledges of allegiance to their lords.

Tolkien also compares and contrasts the lords of Book Five. The evil Germanic lord Denethor is matched by the good Germanic lord Theoden; both contrast with the Christian lord Aragorn. Denethor fails as a father, a master, a steward, and a rational man. In 'The Siege of Gondor' (Chapter Four) and later in 'The Pyre of Denethor' (Chapter Seven) Denethor reveals his inability to love his son Faramir when, Lear-like, he measures the quality and quantity of his worth. He prefers the dead Boromir to Faramir because of the former's great courage and loyalty to him. 'Boromir was loyal to me and no wizard's pupil. He would have remembered his father's need, and would not have squandered what fortune gave. He would have brought me a mighty gift' (III, 104). So he chastises Faramir for his betrayal: 'have I not seen your eye fixed on Mithrandir, seeking whether you said well or too much? He has long had your heart in his keeping' (III, 103). In the early chapters he reveals his failure as a master: he assumes the service of a small individual like Pippin must be domestic and menial in character, involving waiting on him, running errands, entertaining him (III, 96). As a steward of Gondor he fails most egregiously by usurping the role of lord in misguided zeal for power and glory and by using his men to further his own ends. He views this act in monetary terms: the Dark Lord 'uses others as his weapons. So do all great lords, if they are wise, Master Halfling. Or why should I sit here in my tower and think, and watch, and wait, spending even my sons?' (III, 111). Unlike Theoden he remains secure in his tower while his warriors die in the siege of Gondor. Most significantly he fails to exhibit that rational self-control typical of man and often described in the Middle Ages through the metaphor of kingship. Such unnatural behaviour results in despair and irrationality, and he loses his head. When he nurses his madness to suicide and adds even his son Faramir to the pyre he is termed a 'heathen' by Gandalf, like those kings dominated by the Dark

Power, 'slaying themselves in pride and despair, murdering their kin to ease their own death' (III, 157). As he succumbs to his pride he refuses to 'be the dotard chamberlain of an upstart. . . . I will not bow to such a one, last of a ragged house long bereft of lordship and dignity' (III, 158). Symbolically the enemy hurls back the heads of dead soldiers branded with the 'token of the Lidless Eye' to signal the loss of reason and hope – the loss of the 'head' – and the assault of despair on this city and its steward (III, 117).

Theoden and Aragorn epitomise in contrast the good king. As a Germanic king Theoden serves primarily heroically after his contest with Wormtongue, giving leadership in battle and loving and paternal treatment of his warriors outside it, as we have seen with Merry. So he rides at the head of his troop of warriors as they near the city and provides a noble and inspiring example for them to follow:

> Arise, arise . . .
> Fell deeds awake fire and slaughter!
> spear shall be shaken, shield be splintered,
> a sword-day, a red day, ere the sun rises!
> Ride now, ride now! Ride to Gondor!
>
> (III, 137)

The alliterative verse echoes the Old English heroic lines of 'The Battle of Maldon' in both its form and content.

Aragorn differs from Theoden in his role as Christian king because of his moral heroism as a healer rather than his valour as a destroyer. Ioreth, the Gondors' wise-woman, declares *'The hands of the king are the hands of a healer, and so shall the rightful king be known'* (III, 169). In 'The Houses of Healing' (Chapter Eight) Aragorn carries the herb *kingsfoil* to the wounded Faramir, Eowyn, and Merry to revive and awaken each of them in highly symbolic acts. Also known as *athelas*, *kingsfoil* brings 'Life to the dying': its restorative powers, of course, transcend the merely physical. It represents Life itself juxtaposed to Death, similar to the restorative powers of the paradisal Niggle in 'Leaf by Niggle'. Indeed, when he places the leaves in hot water, 'all hearts were lightened. For the fragrance that came to each was like a memory of dewy mornings of unshadowed sun in some land of which the fair world in Spring is itself but a fleeting memory' (III, 1973). In awakening Faramir, Aragorn as well awakens knowledge and love so that he responds in words similar to those of a Christian disciple: 'My lord, you called me. I come. What does the king command?' (III, 173). Instead of responding rationally to the king, Eowyn awakens from her deathlike sleep to enjoy her brother's presence and to mourn her father's death. Merry awakens hungry for supper. The revival of self witnessed in these three incidents symbolises the renewal of the three human faculties, rational, appetitive, and sensitive.

Structurally Tolkien supports his thematic contrasts and parallels. The House of Healing visited in Chapter Eight occurs back-to-back with Chapter Seven's House of the Dead in which Denethor commits fiery suicide. More than physical, his death is chiefly spiritual. Both a spiritual and physical rebirth follow Aragorn's laying on of *kingsfoil* in the House of Healing. But so this ritualistic and epiphanic act readies the narrative for the final symbolic Christian gesture of all the free peoples in the last two chapters. In 'The Last Debate' they decide to sacrifice themselves, if necessary, out of love for their world in the hope that their action will distract Sauron long enough for Sam and Frodo to reach Mount Doom. As an entire community of 'servants' they each alone act as freely, spontaneously, and charitably as did Merry or Eowyn toward Theoden earlier. Aragorn declares that 'As I have begun, so I will go on. . . . Nonetheless I do not yet claim to command any man. Let others choose as they will' (III, 192). Even the title of 'The Last Debate' portrays the egalitarian spirit of the group. In contrast in the last chapter, 'The Black Gate Opens', only one view – that of the Dark Lord, voiced by his Mouth, the Lieutenant – predominates. Sauron too demands not voluntary service but servitude: the Lieutenant 'would be their tyrant and they his slaves' (III, 205). Finally, the arrogance of Sauron's 'Steward' functions antithetically to the humility and love of the good 'servants'. Mocking and demeaning them, he asks if 'any one in this rout' has the 'authority to treat with me? . . . Or indeed with wit to understand me?' (III, 202). His stentorian voice grows louder and more defensive when met with the silence of Aragorn, whom he has described as brigand-like. This attack of the free peoples on the Black Gate of Mordor parallels that of Sauron's orcs on the Gate of Gondor in Chapter Four, but differs in that the former consists not so much of physical attack as a spiritual defence. When the peoples realise the Lieutenant holds Sam's short sword, the grey cloak with its elven brooch, and Frodo's mithril-mail they almost succumb to despair – Sauron's greatest weapon, as witnessed in the siege of Gondor. But Gandalf's steely self-discipline and wisdom so steadies their nerves that they are buoyed by his refusal to submit to the Mouth's insolent terms. Well that he does, for Sauron then surrounds them on all sides, betraying his embassy of peace. They are saved from physical destruction by the eagles as *dei ex machina* and from spiritual destruction by Frodo, Sam, and Gollum as they near Mount Doom in Book Six.

The Ring finally reaches its origin in the first three chapters of Book Six. Initiating the idea of 'Return'[16] this event introduces a tripartite division of the book in narrative and theme. In Chapters Four to Seven Aragorn returns as king of his people, after which his marriage to Arwen, in addition to Faramir's to Eowyn, symbolises the renewal of society through the joining of different species, man and elf, and of different nations, Rohan and Gondor. A later marriage symbolises a more natural form of rejuvenation, for Sam as gardener marries an appropriately named Rosie Cotton to illustrate further the fertility emblazoning the reborn Shire. Finally, in the third part (Chapter Eight) Frodo and his hobbits return to the Shire, where the false 'mayor' Sharkey is ousted and a new one, Sam, elected. In the last chapter Tolkien hints at more supernatural forms of return and rebirth. On one level those chosen few 'return' to the Grey Havens, where they seem to acquire an immortality reminiscent of Christianity. But on another level others of a less spiritual cast must return to the duties of the natural world. So Sam returns at the very end, a 'king' who must continue to serve his 'people', his family, and his 'kingdom', the Shire, by remaining in this world: ' "Well, I'm back," he said' (III, 385).

Throughout the first part of Book Six before the Ring has been returned and Sauron similarly 'returns' to a grey smoke (in contrast to the Grey Havens reached by Frodo and Gandalf at the end), Sam exemplifies the ideal Christian servant to his master Frodo in continuation of the Christian-king-as-servant theme enunciated in the last part. Physically he provides food for Frodo as he weakens, offers him his share of the remaining water, carries him bodily over rough terrain, and lifts his spirits. But spiritually he serves Frodo through the moral character which reveals him to be, as the most insignificant hobbit and character in the epic, the most heroic.[17] He will become an artist by the work's end, but even during the trek across Mordor his sensitivity to spiritual reality is expressed by his understanding of the beauty beneath the appearance of waste, of light beyond darkness, of hope beyond despair.

This insight is triggered by the appearance of a star above: 'The beauty of it smote his heart, as he looked up out of the forsaken land, and hope returned to him. For like a shaft, clear and cold, the thought pierced him that in the end the Shadow was only a small and passing thing: there was light and high beauty for ever beyond its reach. . . . Now, for a moment, his own fate, and even his master's ceased to trouble him' (III, 244). Strangely he remains the only character who has worn the Ring but who is never tempted to acquire it by overpowering his master. Yet like Frodo earlier he refuses to kill the detested Gollum when an opportunity arises because of his empathy for this 'thing lying in the dust, forlorn, ruinous, utterly wretched' (III, 273). Having borne the Ring himself, he finally understands the reason for Gollum's wretchedness. This charitable refusal permits Gollum as a foil for the good servant to serve his master and Middle-earth in the most ironic way imaginable; when Frodo betrays himself enough to keep the Ring at the last moment, Gollum bites off both Ring and finger only to fall into the furnace of Mount Doom, the most ignominious 'servant' finally achieving the coveted role of 'Lord of the Rings', the least dangerous adversary finally felling the most dangerous – Sauron.

In the last two parts the reunion of the entire Fellowship and all the species, the coronation of the king, and the double weddings mark the restoration of harmony and peace to Middle-earth. Symbolically the Eldest of Trees blooms again to replace the barren and withered Tree in the Court of the Fountain (III, 308–9). A new Age – the Age of Man, the fourth Age – begins. Even in the Shire rejuvenation occurs: note the domestic image implied by the title of Chapter Eight, 'The Scouring of the Shire'.

In a social sense the Shire must be washed and purified of the reptilian monsters occupying it. Once Sharkey and Worm have disappeared, Sam the new Mayor as gardener can replenish its natural stores as well. After he plants the seed given him by Galadriel, new trees, including a mallorn with silver bark and gold flowers, burst into bloom in the spring. The lush growth introduces a season or rebirth in Shire year 1420 through sunshine, rain in moderation,

> an air of richness and growth, and a gleam of beauty beyond that of mortal summers that flicker and pass upon this Middle-earth. All the children born or begotten in that year, and there were many, were fair to see and strong, and most of them had a rich

golden hair that had before been rare among hobbits. The fruit was so plentiful that young hobbits very nearly bathed in strawberries and cream. . . . And no one was ill, and everyone was pleased, except those who had to mow the grass. (III, 375)

Sam as gardener becomes a natural artist who fuses together the Niggle and Parish of 'Leaf by Niggle'.

The ending of this epic may seem optimistic. But as the Second Age has passed into the Third, so now the Third passes into the Fourth, a lesser one because dominated by man, a lesser species than the elf. Also, as Sauron replaced Morgoth, perhaps an even Darker Lord will replace Sauron in the future. Yet Tolkien's major interest does not lie in predicting the future or in encouraging man to hope for good fortune. He wishes to illustrate how best to conduct man's life, both privately and publicly, by being a good servant and a good king, despite the vagaries of fortune, the corruption of others, and the threat of natural and supernatural death.

So this epic constitutes a sampler of Tolkienian concepts and forms realised singly and separately in other works. The critic as monster depicted in the *Beowulf* article reappears as Tolkien the Critic in the foreword to *The Lord of the Rings*, a 'grown up' version of Tolkien the narrator in *The Hobbit*. The hero as monster finds expression, as it has earlier in Bilbo, in Frodo, who discovers the landscape of the self to be a harsher terrain than that of Mordor. The series of monsters typifying the deadly sins – Saruman, Shelob – ultimately converge with the evil Germanic king of the trilogy – Denethor – combining ideas of the 'King under the Mountain' in *The Hobbit* with the idea of the Germanic king presented in 'The Homecoming' and other medieval parodies. The good Germanic hero-as-subordinate, too, from *The Hobbit* and the medieval parodies, converges with the Christian concept of the king-as-servant from the fairy-stories, in the last two volumes of the trilogy. In addition the genres and formal constructs Tolkien most loves reappear here. The preface, lecture, or prose non-fiction essay is transformed into the Foreword; the 'children's story' for adults is expanded into the adult story of the epic, also for children; the parody of medieval literature recurs not only in the epic or romance form used here but also in the presentation of the communities of Rohan and Gondor; the fairy-story with its secondary world of Faërie governed by a very Christian Elf-king is translated into elven form here. Thus all of Tolkien's work manifests a unity, with understanding of its double and triple levels, in this respect like the distinct dual levels, Germanic and Christian, of *Beowulf* first perceived in Tolkien's own *Beowulf* article. So the Tolkien reader, like Bilbo in *The Hobbit* and Sam in *The Lord of the Rings*, must return to the beginning – not to the Shire, but to the origin of the artist Tolkien – in 'Beowulf: The Monsters and the Critics'.

Conclusion: *The Silmarillion*—Tolkien's 'Book of Lost Tales'

The Silmarillion is a lost book in a double sense. Originally entitled 'The Book of Lost Tales', as if it had been lost and then discovered as a 'mythology *for England*',[1] it represents yet another attempt by Tolkien to pretend that he is the editor or translator of works belonging to a previous era, as he has done in *Farmer Giles of Ham*, *The Adventures of Tom Bombadil*, and *The Lord of the Rings* (especially in the Foreword and Appendices), even though in this case the mock-Preface and editorial apparatus are missing. But it is a lost book in a second sense, in that it was never completed in the sixty years between its inception in 1914 and his death in 1973. The present text resulted from his son Christopher's posthumous revision and editing of a work complicated to begin with, but which in addition existed in multiple versions, and often versions differing in detail from each other and from *The Lord of the Rings* (chapters on Galadriel and the ents had to be added for this reason).[2] Thus any critical study must be prefaced with this important *caveat*: we do not know exactly what Tolkien's final intentions were.

The work was never completed within Tolkien's lifetime for a variety of reasons. By 1923 'The Book of Lost Tales' was nearly finished but instead of ending it with the Earendel voyage as he had planned he rewrote it.[3] During his busy career he continued to revise and rewrite it; even after his retirement from Oxford its completion continued to be interrupted by proofs to be read, letters to be written, earlier publications to be revised, and translations he wished to publish. It had been submitted to his publishers as a possible successor to the popular *Hobbit* in 1937, but Stanley Unwin declined to publish it, for it 'is a mine to be explored in writing further books like *The Hobbit* rather than a book in itself'.[4] And when at the age of sixty Tolkien wanted to publish it together with the recently completed *Lord of the Rings*, Raynor Unwin, Stanley's son, objected: 'surely this is a case for an editor who would incorporate any *really* relevant material from *The Silmarillion* into *The Lord of the Rings* without increasing the already enormous bulk of the latter and, if feasible, even cutting it.'[5]

Even now in its published form *The Silmarillion* is difficult to read and even more difficult to enjoy. Despite its epic theme the collection still lacks continuity, if not unity, and is hard to follow. Each of its five parts relates the history and genealogy of one or more species in the order of their creation through various tales – those of the Ainur, Valar, elves, dwarves, and men. 'Ainulindale' ('The Music of the Ainur') and 'Valaquenta' ('Account of the Valar and Maiar') briefly outline the creation of the Ainur (or Valar to the elves, gods to men) by the One and summarise their individual characters. The third and longest part, 'Quenta Silmarillion' ('The History of the Silmarils') in its twenty-four chapters deals with the history of those beings created by the One, the immortal elves and mortal men granted the gift of death, and the beings created by Aulë of the Valar, the dwarves. The last two parts record the downfall of man, of the noblest tribe of men in 'Akallâbeth' ('The Downfall of Númenor'), and of the lesser tribes in 'Of the Rings of Power and the Third Age'. Although the collection dramatises the history of Middle-earth (from the Old English phrase for 'Earth' derived from Old Norse) from the beginning of Creation to the point at which *The Hobbit* and *The Lord of the Rings* end, it lacks a central epic hero who could pull together the various strands of the narrative. Possibly Tolkien himself realised its lack of focus, for he originally intended that these tales be framed by 'the introductory device of the seafarer to whom the stories were told'.[6]

A second problem with this mythological work is its plethora of names of peoples, individuals, and places (the 'Index of Names' supplied by Christopher at the end lists an appalling eight to nine hundred, many of which are mentioned only once in this three-hundred-page work). Tolkien's interest in philology nearly adumbrates the work as a fictional narrative. Like Morgoth and Fëanor in *The Silmarillion*, Tolkien seems to love what he has created as an end in itself, and the ensuing catalogue of names confuses, if not stifles, the reader, as one example will attest:

> At length the Vanyar and the Noldor came over Ered Luin, the Blue Mountains, between Eriador and the westernmost land of Middle-earth, which the Elves after named Beleriand; and the foremost companies passed over the Vale of Sirion and came down to the shores of the Great Sea between Drengist and the Bay of Balar. . . . And the host of the Teleri passed over the Misty Mountains, and crossed the wide lands of Eriador, being urged on by Elwë Singollo, for he was eager to return to Valinor.[7]

Despite Christopher's helpful aids to readers included at the work's end – the genealogical tables, Index of Names, Notes on Pronunciation, an appendix on 'Elements on Quenya and Sindarin Names', and two maps – the love of private language is here almost too private for the general reader to share.

Thus *The Silmarillion* becomes a 'lost book' in a third sense, in that as a work of fiction it remains so dominated by philology that it is nearly reduced to the state of a dictionary or encyclopaedia of words and myths. Given these objections, however, Christopher has provided a major service to Tolkien fans and scholars by editing this 'compendious narrative', as he terms it in his Foreword. Interesting bits of information surface: it is revealed that Gandalf possessed one of the three elven rings, along with Elrond and Galadriel. And the story of Beren and Lúthien, whom Tolkien identified as himself and his wife Edith, possesses biographical as well as literary interest. Not a unified novel like *The Hobbit* or the 'three-decker novel' of the trilogy, the 'prose poem' has an air of authenticity and reads like the Elder Edda. Thus as a mythological work constructed along the lines of a genealogy of created beings it resembles other collections of mythological tales, often beginning with Creation – like the Bible, Ovid's *Metamorphoses*, Hyginus' *Fabulae*, the Eddas, the Welsh *Mabinogion*, the Irish myths and legends of the hero Cuchulain.

As a mythological work its epic conflicts, themes, and symbols relate to those analysed in the preceding chapters on fictional and non-fiction works. Specifically Tolkien reworks religious concepts and symbols into his invented legends, as he has in previous works – the theme of pride and fall, related to the desire for power over others as symbolised in the role of the king or wise leader, and knowledge as an end in itself as symbolised in skilfully worked material objects loved for themselves. Although Tolkien contrasts with this the regenerative powers of art as he has in other works, in this collection however there is no Christian king, healer, or artist as in the fairy-stories, *The Hobbit*, or *The Lord of the Rings*. Instead a much more Old Testament emphasis predominates: it is the art of the Creator, Eru the One, which is celebrated at beginning and end, and the promise of natural and spiritual renewal for all of creation upon the fulfilment of obedience to the will of the One. Nor is there the specifically medieval English emphasis on the chivalric concept of the lord or knight using his own men to establish his reputation, or the Old English concept of the loyal warrior as good servant. The development of strong fictional characters here gives way to the importance of theme, image, idea in the cycle of myths.

Basically the mythology dramatises the conflict between the fallen Vala Melkor, or Morgoth, followed by his Maia servant Sauron and the One, Eru or Ilúvatar, 'Father of All', although this is not at first apparent because of the bewildering array of tales and characters. At the beginning Melkor, conceived like the other Ainur as a 'thought' of the One, rebels against him. The most talented of the Ainur, Melkor refuses to sing his part in their cosmic music because 'desire grew hot within him to bring into Being things of his own' (p. 16). He creates in his own music a loud, vain 'clamorous unison as of many trumpets braying upon a few notes' instead of the slow, beautiful, sorrowful music of the One. Yet both clamorous and beautiful pieces are translated by Eru into a created world and its inhabitants so that even Melkor and his discord find a part. Melkor's later 'offspring' indeed resemble him spiritually: Fëanor as the greatest of the elven tribe of the Noldor also wishes like the Valar to create 'things of his own' and he learns through the art of Melkor how to capture the blessed light of the Two Trees (made by the Vala Yavanna) in three jewels, the Silmarils. Like Melkor he too succumbs to a 'greedy love' of them that leads to his and his son's downfall. In the next-to-last section of *The Silmarillion*, Ar-Pharazôn, mightiest and proudest of the Númenóreans, themselves noblest of men, calls himself 'The Golden' and wishes to be king, for 'his heart was filled with the desire of power unbounded and the sole dominion of his will. And he determined without counsel of the Valar, or any wisdom but his own, that the title of King of Men he would himself claim, and would compel Sauron to become his vassal and his servant; for in his pride he deemed that no king should ever arise so mighty as to vie with the Heir of Eärendil' (p. 270). He rebels against the elves and Valar as Melkor earlier had rebelled against the One. In the last section even the Maia Sauron desires to control Middle-earth out of a similar pride and envy, and he fashions the One Ring to do so, itself a created thing misused by its creator like the three elven jewels of Fëanor.

Despite the ensuing fall of elves and men and the destruction of Middle-earth, 'peace came again, and a new Spring opened on earth; and the Heir of Isildur was crowned King of Gondor and Arnor, and the might of the Dúnedain was lifted up and their glory renewed' (p. 304), with the beginning of the Fourth Age, of Man. Evil stands revealed as only a part of the whole goodness of Creation perceived by the One Himself, and Himself alone. So the 'secret thoughts' of Melkor's mind – his pride, envy, greed, hatred – formed 'but a part of the whole and tributary to its glory' (p. 17), as Eru had explained to him even before Middle-earth was created. The central message of *The Silmarillion* emerges from the ruin and sorrow as delivered by the prophetic Messenger sent by the Valar to warn Men: 'Beware! The will of Eru may not be gainsaid; and the Valar bid you earnestly not to withhold the trust to which you are called, lest it become again a bond by which you are constrained. . . . The love of Arda [Middle-earth] was set in your hearts by Ilúvatar, and he does not plant to no purpose' (p. 265). Love and trust, not pride and wilfulness, are the key words.

The theme of good and evil that derives from the conflict between Melkor and the One is underscored by music and jewel symbolism. 'The Silmarillion' entitles the whole collection and not just the long middle section describing the history of the three jewels in part because it complements the companion epic-novels of *The Lord of the Rings* with their ring symbolism. In part, too, it helps to unify the entire mythology: the Silmarils, like the music of Melkor dominating the first part and the Ring of Sauron dominating the fifth, are created things misused by their creators and like them they symbolise the domination of will that springs from pride and greed, the chief elements of selfishness. After creating the jewels in order to preserve the light of the two Trees, the glory of the Blessed Realm, Fëanor 'began to love the Silmarils with a greedy love, and grudged the sight of them to all save his father and his seven sons; he seldom remembered now that the light within them was not his own' (p. 69). Melkor too of course burns with the desire to possess them; the greed of both leads to alienation from others, division among family and nation, and much destruction. The jewels are cursed with an oath of hatred, so that when the dwarves later behold the Silmaril set in the necklace named Nauglamír 'they were filled with a great lust to possess them, and carry them off to their far homes in the mountains' (p. 233). One should not imitate the Creator in order to aggrandise creation for selfish reasons, but instead to praise both Creator and creation, to reflect one's love for and trust in both and one's obedience to the will of Ilúvatar. Such purpose advances under- standing and promotes healing. For the beauty created by the artist reflects only the beauty of the larger creation, and not the greatness of its creator. It is no mistake that this work begins with the words 'There was Eru, the One', and concludes with the words 'story and song'. Because these tales celebrate the power of creation and goodness through the image of song, music, and its triumph over destruction and evil as represented by broken and inharmonious song, this very 'Book of Lost Tales' might be viewed as itself a praise of creation – and creativity.

The themes of the work can be seen as clearly biblical. The conflict between Melkor, or Morgoth (and his spiritual descen- dants), and the One or the creation of the One mirrors that between God and the fallen angel Satan; his corruption of the 'third theme' of creation, of the elves and men, mirrors that of Adam and Eve by Satan; the desire for power and godlike being is the same desire for knowledge of good and evil witnessed in the Garden of Eden. As symbols of such desire the Silmarils and One Ring show that pride as chief of the deadly sins leads to envy, covetousness, and, in the figure of the giant spider Ungoliant, companion of Morgoth, gluttony and lust. For this reason dark becomes an appropriate image to associate with monstrosity, and light with good. Men see death, for example, as a curse because 'coming under the shadow of Morgoth it seemed to them that they were surrounded by a great darkness, of which they were afraid; and some grew wilful and proud and would not yield, until life was reft from them' (p. 256).

Tolkien's triumph in this last but first work then lies not only in its creation of a whole history (and in a sense morality) for Middle-earth, providing thereby a context for *The Hobbit* and *The*

Lord of the Rings. For, when Christopher in the Foreword claims that this 'compendious narrative' of mythological tales was 'made long afterward from sources of great diversity (poems and annals, and oral tales) that had survived in agelong tradition', one is not sure whether he is describing the literary output of one man, or of one *nation*. Perhaps Christopher merely means to agree that, in Tolkien's fantasy mythology for Middle-earth, he has indeed finally written that 'mythology *for England*'.

Notes

INTRODUCTION

1. *Letters*, ed. W. H. Lewis (1966; rpt. New York and London: Harcourt Brace Jovanovich, 1975).
2. Randel Helms, *Tolkien's World* (Boston: Houghton Mifflin, 1974) pp. 1–2.
3. Humphrey Carpenter, *J. R. R. Tolkien: A Biography* (London, Boston, and Sydney: Allen & Unwin, 1977) p. 75.
4. Carpenter, pp. 89–90.
5. Carpenter, pp. 59, 71, 89, 94.
6. Carpenter, pp. 64, 71.
7. These dates exist in pencilled notes by Tolkien on a letter of 18 January 1938 from G. H. White of the Examination Schools, which was exhibited in the 'Oxford Writers' exhibit at Oxford University in March 1978.
8. Christopher Tolkien, Foreword, in J. R. R. Tolkien, *The Silmarillion*, ed. Christopher Tolkien (London: Allen & Unwin; Boston: Houghton Mifflin, 1977) p. 7.
9. The lecture was published in *Proceedings of the British Academy*, 22 (1936) 245–95, and reprinted in *An Anthology of Beowulf Criticism*, ed. Lewis E. Nicholson (Notre Dame, Indiana: University of Notre Dame Press, 1963) pp. 51–103; and also in *The Beowulf Poet*, ed. Donald K. Fry (Englewood Cliffs, New Jersey: Prentice-Hall, 1968) pp. 8–56.

CHAPTER 1

1. Randel Helms, *Tolkien's World* (Boston: Houghton Mifflin, 1974) pp. 2–7, does discuss briefly the impact of the article on Tolkien's development of a theory of fantasy: 'In the lecture we see him, perhaps almost without realizing it, identify himself with the *Beowulf* poet and in his own defense, as it were, provide telling critical justifications for ancient poetic strategies he was even then reviving in his own work' (p. 2). However, he does not perceive the critic as a monster, proceed further in analysing the article, or trace its impact on Tolkien's fiction. In addition, although she ignores the *Beowulf* article *per se*, Bonniejean Christensen does compare the poem *Beowulf* to *The Hobbit*: see '*Beowulf* and *The Hobbit*: Elegy into Fantasy in J. R. R. Tolkien's Creative Technique', Diss. University of Southern

California, 1969; see also the article derived from the dissertation, 'Tolkien's Creative Technique: *Beowulf* and *The Hobbit*', *Orcrist*, 7 (1972–73) 16–20; finally her 'Gollum's Character Transformation in *The Hobbit*', *A Tolkien Compass*, ed. Jared Lobdell (La Salle, Ill.: Open Court Press, 1975) pp. 9–28, mentions, in passing, the parallel between *Beowulf* and *The Hobbit*.

2. Beowulf: The Monsters and the Critics', *Proceedings of the British Academy*, 22 (1936) 245–95, rpt. in *An Anthology of Beowulf Criticism*, ed. Lewis E. Nicholson (Notre Dame: University of Notre Dame Press, 1963) pp. 51–104, and in *The Beowulf Poet*, ed. Donald K. Fry (Englewood Cliffs, New Jersey: Prentice-Hall, 1968) pp. 8–56. All citations refer to the Nicholson reprint (this reference, p. 51).

3. 'On Fairy-Stories', in *Tree and Leaf* (London: Allen & Unwin, 1964; Boston: Houghton Mifflin, 1965) p. 3, rpt. in *The Tolkien Reader* (1966; rpt. New York: Ballantine, 1975).

4. *Farmer Giles of Ham* (London: Allen & Unwin, 1949; Boston: Houghton Mifflin, 1950) p. 7, rpt. in *The Tolkien Reader*.

5. Foreword, *The Lord of the Rings* (rev. ed., New York: Ballantine, 1965) 3 vols, I, ix.

6. J. R. R. Tolkien and E. V. Gordon (eds), *Sir Gawain and the Green Knight*, 2nd ed. rev. Norman Davis (1967; rpt. pb. Oxford: Clarendon Press, 1967) p. vii.

7. Prefatory Note, *The English Text of the Ancrene Riwle: Ancrene Wisse*, Early English Text Society N.S. No. 249 (London, New York, and Toronto: Oxford University Press, 1962) pp. vi–viii.

8. P. vii. Note the similarity to the comments in the Introduction, *Sir Gawain and the Green Knight, Pearl, and Sir Orfeo*, trans. J. R. R. Tolkien (London: Allen & Unwin, 1975; Boston: Houghton Mifflin, 1975) p. 17. Ignoring discussions of the sources of *Sir Gawain* largely because there are no direct ones, Tolkien declares, 'For that reason, since I am speaking of this poem and this author, and not of ancient rituals, nor of pagan divinities of the Sun, nor of Fertility, nor of the Dark and the Underworld, in the almost wholly lost antiquity of the North and of these Western Isles – as remote from Sir Gawain of Camelot as the gods of the Aegean are from Troilus and Pandarus in Chaucer – for that reason I have not said anything about the story, or stories, that the author used.' Of course, in this very long denial he has said quite a lot.

9. Preface, *The Ancrene Riwle*, trans. M. B. Salu (London: Burns & Oates, 1955) p. v.

10. Prefatory Remarks, *Beowulf and the Finnesburg Fragment*, trans. John R. Clark Hall (1940; rev. ed. 1950; rpt. London: Allen & Unwin, 1972) p. x.

11. '*Ancrene Wisse* and *Hali Meiðhad*', *Essays and Studies by Members of the English Association*, 14 (1929) 104. For similar expressions of his interest in Old and Middle English philology and linguistics see *A Middle English Vocabulary* (Oxford: Clarendon Press, 1922); 'Some Contributions to Middle-English Lexicography', *Review of English Studies*, 1 (1925) 210–15; 'The Devil's Coach-Horses', *Review of English Studies*, 1 (1925) 331–6; Foreword to *A New Glossary of the Dialect of the Huddersfield District* by Walter E. Haigh (London: Oxford University Press, 1928) pp. xiii–xviii;

'Sigelwara Land', Part 1, in *Medium Aevum*, 1 (1932) 183–96, and Part 2 in *Medium Aevum*, 3 (1934) 95–111; 'Chaucer as Philologist: The Reeve's Tale', *Transactions of the Philological Society* (1934) pp. 1–70; and 'Middle English "Losenger": Sketch of an Etymological and Semantic Enquiry', in *Essais de Philologie Moderne* (Paris: Société d'édition 'Les Belles Lettres', 1953) 63–76.

12. *The Adventures of Tom Bombadil* (London: Allen & Unwin, 1962; Boston: Houghton Mifflin, 1962) p. 7, rpt. in *The Tolkien Reader*.

13. For a discussion of the enormous time and energy Tolkien devoted to his teaching, research, and other professional responsibilities see Humphrey Carpenter, *J. R. R. Tolkien: A Biography* (London, Boston, and Sydney: Allen & Unwin, 1977) pp. 131–42.

14. *The Two Towers; being the second part of The Lord of the Rings* (London: Allen & Unwin, 1955; Boston: Houghton Mifflin, 1956, rev. ed. 1965; rpt. pb. New York: Ballantine, 1965) p. 204.

15. Tolkien in the Introductory Note, *Tree and Leaf*, claims the essay and tale are linked for three reasons: their common leaf/tree symbolism, their interest in the theme of sub-creation, and their dates of origin, 1938–9, concurrent with the beginning of *The Lord of the Rings* (p. 2).

16. In the second volume of *The Lord of the Rings* Saruman similarly destroys the trees of Fangorn – which he does not own – to use the wood in scientific experiments and to build machines of destruction, an act that provokes the wrath of the ents and thus leads to his 'fall', as they attack and imprison him, symbolically, in 'Cunning Mind', Orthanc.

17. See, for example, *Cursor Mundi*, ed. Rev. Richard Morris, Early English Text Society, O.S. No. 57, 59, 62, 66, 68, 99, 101 (London: K. Paul, Trench, Trübner, 1874–93) pp. 84–6. For other medieval descriptions of the Tree, see Morton W. Bloomfield, *The Seven Deadly Sins: An Introduction to the History of a Religious Concept* (East Lansing: Michigan State College, 1952).

18. St Augustine, *On Christian Doctrine*, trans. D. W. Robertson, Jr. (Indianapolis and New York: Bobbs-Merrill, 1958) p. 51 (2.16).

19. Macrobius in his fourth-century commentary on the *Somnium Scipionis*, an extremely influential work in the Middle Ages, described fabulous narrative as the truth 'treated in a fictitious style', or 'a decent and dignified conception of holy truths, with respectable events and characters, . . . presented beneath a modest veil of allegory'. Such a style must be employed because 'a frank, open exposition of herself is distasteful to Nature, who, just as she has withheld an understanding of herself from the uncouth senses of men by enveloping herself in variegated garments, has also desired to have her secrets handled by more prudent individuals through fabulous narratives'. See Macrobius' *Commentary on the Dream of Scipio*, trans. William Harris Stahl (1952; rpt. New York and London: Columbia University Press, 1966) pp. 85–6 (1.2.10–11 and 17). 'Allegory' was also regarded by poets as a kind of 'cover' or 'cloak' for bare truth in the twelfth century: see the discussion of *integumentum* in Winthrop Wetherbee, *Platonism and Poetry in the Twelfth Century: The Literary Influence of the School of Chartres* (Princeton: Princeton University Press, 1972) esp. pp. 36–73.

20. See, e.g., John Conley (ed.), *The Middle English Pearl: Critical Essays*

(Notre Dame and London: University of Notre Dame Press, 1970).

21. Letter to Fr. Peter Milward, 10 December 1956, in *Letters of C. S. Lewis*, ed. W. H. Lewis (1966; rpt. New York and London: Harcourt Brace Jovanovich, 1975) p. 273.

22. For example, Lionel S. Lewis, *Scaling the Ivory Tower: Merit and Its Limits in Academic Careers* (Baltimore and London: Johns Hopkins University Press, 1975) pp. 1–2, 4–6, traces back the history of the American university split between the Germanic research university and the English teaching college to the mid-nineteenth century, when the Teutonic presence first asserted itself in the institution.

23. Carpenter admits: 'There were not two Tolkien's, one an academic and the other a writer. They were the same man, and the two sides of him overlapped so that they were indistinguishable – or rather they were not two sides at all, but different expressions of the same mind, the same imagination, (p. 131). For the two sides of his personality, one public and cheerful, one private and pessimistic, which apparently developed after the death of his mother, see p. 31.

CHAPTER 2

1. See, for example, Mary R. Lucas, Review of *The Hobbit* in *Library Journal*, 63 (1 May 1938) 385: 'It will have a limited appeal unless properly introduced and even then will be best liked by those children whose imagination is alert.' Very recently Randel Helms viewed it as intended 'for children and filled with a whimsy few adults can accept', in *Tolkien's World* (Boston: Houghton Mifflin, 1974) p. 19.

2. For a discussion of the children's story elements, primarily the narrative intrusions, plus those episodes which foreshadow incidents in *The Lord of the Rings* (a work which in contrast 'stretches the adult imagination', p. 19), see Paul H. Kocher, *Master of Middle-earth: The Fiction of J. R. R. Tolkien* (Boston: Houghton Mifflin, 1972) pp. 19–33. A similar awareness of the awkward mixture of the two levels is expressed by Bonniejean Christensen, 'Gollum's Character Transformation in *The Hobbit*', in *A Tolkien Compass*, ed. Jared Lobdell (La Salle, Ill.: Open Court Press, 1975) pp. 9–28: the alterations in the character of Gollum between the edition of 1937 and that of 1951 'clearly increase Gollum's role and remove the story from the realm of the nursery tale', p. 27, in preparation for his 'expanded role' later in *The Lord of the Rings*.

3. Dorothy Matthews, 'The Psychological Journey of Bilbo Baggins', in *A Tolkien Compass*, pp. 29–42, views Bilbo's maturation in Jungian terms; Helms, pp. 41–55, interprets it in Freudian terms, and the whole work, in addition, as a microcosm of *The Lord of the Rings* (pp. 19–40).

4. J. R. R. Tolkien, quoted by Philip Norman in 'The Prevalence of Hobbits', *The New York Times Magazine* (15 Jan 1967), p. 100.

5. Tolkien critics have, curiously, ignored his own *Beowulf* article as a possible parallel to *The Hobbit* although they have adduced parallels between the novel and *Beowulf* or other medieval works. See Bonniejean Christensen, '*Beowulf* and *The Hobbit*: Elegy into Fantasy in J. R. R. Tolkien's Creative Technique', *DAI*, 30 (1970) 4401A–4402A (University of Southern California), and the article derived from the dissertation, 'Tol-

kien's Creative Technique: Beowulf and The Hobbit', Orcrist, 7 (1972–73) 16–20, in which The Hobbit is interpreted as a retelling of Beowulf 'from a Christian rather than a pagan point of view', p. 16. Christensen uses Klaeber's idea of the poem's structure rather than Tolkien's to show that Beowulf's four sections (comprising the monsters, the descendants of Cain, the episodes and digressions, and the Dragon) parallel The Hobbit's. The result is that Grendel in Beowulf occupies the same structural position as the trolls and goblins in the first section of The Hobbit, and Unferth and Grendel's Mother the same position as Gollum in the second section. For another view of The Hobbit as four-part in structure see also William Howard Green, 'The Hobbit and Other Fiction by J. R. R. Tolkien: Their ·Roots in Medieval Heroic Literature and Language', DAI, 30 (1970) 4944A (Louisiana State University). Green catalogues medieval analogues for The Hobbit's characters, events and symbols; his work, like Christensen's, is important because it reveals Tolkien's indebtedness to medieval literature in The Hobbit and other works.

6. According to pencilled notes by Tolkien on a letter of 18 January 1938 from G. H. White of the Examination Schools (exhibited at the 'Oxford Writers' exhibit at Oxford University in March 1978), he began writing The Hobbit after he moved to 20 Northmoor Road in 1931, although his children had heard some episodes from it before 1930. The typescript (except the last chapters) was shown to Tolkien in 1932, and the work was retyped for Allen & Unwin in 1936. However, in a letter to the Observer on 20 February 1938 (p. 9), Tolkien admits that for The Hobbit 'Beowulf is among my most valued sources; though it was not consciously present to the mind in the process of writing, in which the episode of the theft arose naturally (and almost inevitably) from the circumstances'. He also admits that 'My tale is not consciously based on any other book – save one, and that is unpublished: the "Silmarillion", a history of the Elves, to which frequent allusion is made'.

7. 'Beowulf: The Monsters and the Critics', Proceedings of the British Academy, 22 (1936) 245–95, rpt. in An Anthology of Beowulf Criticism, ed. Lewis E. Nicholson (Notre Dame: University of Notre Dame Press, 1963) pp. 51–103, and in The Beowulf Poet, ed. Donald K. Fry (Englewood Cliffs, New Jersey: Prentice-Hall, 1968) pp. 8–56. All citations refer to the Nicholson reprint (here, p. 76, n 23).

8. Levin L. Schücking, 'Das Königsideal im Beowulf', MHRA Bulletin, 3 (1929) 143–54, rpt. and trans. as 'The Ideal of Kingship in Beowulf' in Nicholson, pp. 35–49.

9. Tolkien discusses the dialectical features of this work in 'Ancrene Wisse and Hali Meiðhad', Essays and Studies by Members of the English Association, 14 (1929) 104–26; applauds the translation of The Ancrene Riwle by M. B. Salu (London: Burns & Oates, 1955), in his preface to it (p. v); and himself edits The English Text of the Ancrene Riwle: Ancrene Wisse for the Early English Text Society, No. 249 (London, New York, and Toronto: Oxford University Press, 1962).

10. Tolkien describes the poem as 'a contrasted description of two moments in a great life, rising and setting; an elaboration of the ancient and intensely moving contrast between youth and age, first achievement

and final death. It is divided in consequence into two opposed portions, different in matter, manner, and length: A from 1 to 2199 (including an exordium of 52 lines); B from 2200 to 3182 (the end)', Nicholson, p. 81.

11. On eucatastrophe and fantasy see 'On Fairy-Stories', in *Tree and Leaf* (London: Allen & Unwin, 1964; Boston: Houghton Mifflin, 1965) pp. 68–73, rpt. in *The Tolkien Reader* (1966; rpt. New York: Ballantine, 1975). On *Beowulf* as an elegy see 'Beowulf: The Monsters and the Critics', p. 85. See also Christensen, 'Tolkien's Creative Technique', p. 16.

12. *The Hobbit; or There and Back Again* (London: Allen & Unwin, 1937, 1951; Boston: Houghton Mifflin, 1938, 1958; New York: Ballantine, 1965, rpt. 1974) p. 83.

13. Kocher, pp. 19–23.

CHAPTER 3

1. Mrs Sherwood (ed.) *The Governess, or The Little Female Academy* (1820), cited in Gillian Avery, *Nineteenth-Century Children: Heroes and Heroines in English Children's Stories 1780–1900* (London: Hodder & Stoughton, 1965) p. 41.

2. According to the Editorial, p. 6 of *Redbook* (Dec 1967), wherein 'Smith' was first published (pp. 58–61, 101, 103–7). Also in *Smith of Wootton Major and Farmer Giles of Ham.* (London: Allen & Unwin, 1967; Boston: Houghton Mifflin, 1967; New York: Ballantine Books, 1969; rpt. 1975).

3. Randel Helms, *Tolkien's World* (Boston: Houghton Mifflin, 1974) p. 118.

4. Paul Kocher, *Master of Middle-Earth: The Fiction of J. R. R. Tolkien* (Boston: Houghton Mifflin, 1972) pp. 161–9.

5. For 'Leaf' see Helms, pp. 110–18 and Kocher, pp. 144–51; for 'Smith' see Kocher, pp. 173–81.

6. Helms, pp. 119–25: Smith is Tolkien, the Master Cook resembles Bilbo. As Tolkien in 1949 would have been 57, on completing *The Lord of the Rings* in that same year he might have felt ready to relinquish his artistic 'gift'.

7. Tolkien, cited by Philip Norman, 'The Prevalence of Hobbits', *The New York Times Magazine* (15 Jan 1967) p. 100.

8. 'Beowulf: The Monsters and the Critics', *Proceedings of the British Academy*, 22 (1936) 245–95; rpt. in *An Anthology of Beowulf Criticism*, ed. Lewis E. Nicholson (Notre Dame: University of Notre Dame Press, 1963) pp. 51–103; and in *The Beowulf Poet*, ed. Donald K. Fry (Englewood Cliffs, New Jersey: Prentice-Hall, 1968) pp. 8–56. All references derive from the Nicholson anthology.

9. 'On Fairy-Stories', *Essays Presented to Charles Williams*, ed. C. S. Lewis (London: Oxford University Press, 1947; Grand Rapids, Michigan: William B. Eerdmans, 1966); rev. and rpt. in *Tree and Leaf* (London: Allen & Unwin, 1964; Boston: Houghton Mifflin, 1965) p. 66; rpt. in *The Tolkien Reader* (New York: Ballantine, 1966; rpt. 1975). All references derive from *The Tolkien Reader* (p. 67 for this citation).

10. *The Ancrene Riwle*, trans. M. B. Salu (London: Burns & Oates, 1955) p. 173.

11. See Etienne Gilson, *Reason and Revelation in the Middle Ages* (1938; rpt. New York: Charles Scribner's Sons, 1966).

12. See Bonniejean Christensen, '*Beowulf* and *The Hobbit*: Elegy into

Fantasy in J. R. R. Tolkien's Creative Technique', *DAI*, 30 (1970) 4401A–4402A (University of Southern California); and the article derived from the dissertation, 'Tolkien's Creative Technique: *Beowulf* and *The Hobbit'*, *Orcrist*, 7 (1972–73) 16–20.

13. 'Leaf by Niggle', *Dublin Review*, 216 (1945) 46–61, rpt. in *Tree and Leaf*; and in *The Tolkien Reader* (p. 104).

14. See especially D. W. Robertson, Jr., 'The Doctrine of Charity in Mediaeval Literary Gardens: A Topical Approach through Symbolism and Allegory', *Speculum,* 26 (1951) rpt. in *An Anthology of Beowulf Criticism,* ed. Nicholson, pp. 165–88, but esp. pp. 168–73.

15. Macrobius' *Commentary on the Dream of Scipio*, trans. William Harris Stahl (1952; rpt. New York and London: Columbia University Press, 1966) p. 131. But see also pp. 128ff.

16. In his twelfth-century commentary on the first six books of the *Aeneid*, Bernardus Silvestris describes this Neo-Platonic version of the over- and underworld. See my *Genius Figure in Antiquity and the Middle Ages* (New York and London: Columbia University Press, 1975) pp. 43–5.

17. Reprinted in *Smith of Wootton Major and Farmer Giles of Ham* (New York: Ballantine, 1969; rpt. 1975) p. 21.

CHAPTER 4

1. 'The Lay of Aotrou and Itroun', *Welsh Review*, 4 (1945) 254–66. See Paul Kocher's discussion of the work in *Master of Middle-earth: The Fiction of J. R. R. Tolkien* (Boston: Houghton Mifflin, 1972) pp. 169–78. Curiously, he terms it a 'fairy-tale tragedy', ignoring both its medieval genre and Tolkien's own definition of 'fairy-tale' and 'tragedy'. See also, for this poem and others, George Burke Johnston, 'The Poetry of J. R. R. Tolkien', in 'The Tolkien Papers', *Mankato Studies in English*, 2 (1967) 63–75.

2. *Farmer Giles of Ham* (London: Allen & Unwin, 1949; Boston: Houghton Mifflin, 1950); rpt. in *The Tolkien Reader* (New York: Ballantine, 1966; rpt. 1975); and in *Smith of Wootton Major and Farmer Giles of Ham* (New York: Ballantine, 1969; rpt. 1975). All references to *Farmer Giles* derive from *The Tolkien Reader* reprinting. For a discussion of its genre see J. A. Johnson, '*Farmer Giles of Ham:* What is it?' *Orcrist*, 7 (1972–73) 21–4. He adds epic to *fabliau* and romance and also sees in it echoes of the Icelandic saga, the chronicle, and the fable.

3. 'The Homecoming of Beorhtnoth Beorhthelm's Son', *Essays and Studies by Members of the English Association*, N.S. 6 (1953) 1–18; rpt. in *The Tolkien Reader*. See Tolkien's prefatory comments on its verse form, p. 5, and his concluding gloss on its genre, p. 19.

4. 'Imram', *Time and Tide*, 36 (1955) 1561. For a fine analysis of the poem and a comparison with its source see Kocher, pp. 204–12. For a brief history of this source in the Middle Ages see George Boas, *Essays on Primitivism and Related Ideas in the Middle Ages* (Baltimore: Johns Hopkins University Press, 1948) pp. 158–9.

5. *The Adventures of Tom Bombadil* (London: Allen & Unwin, 1962; Boston: Houghton Mifflin, 1962); rpt. in *The Tolkien Reader*. For a discussion of 'scholarly parody' in this work see Randel Helms, *Tolkien's World* (Boston: Houghton Mifflin, 1974) pp. 126–47.

6. On medieval ideas in *The Hobbit* see for example Bonniejean Christensen's '*Beowulf* and *The Hobbit*: Elegy into Fantasy in J. R. R. Tolkien's Creative Technique', *DAI*, 30 (1970) 4401A–4402A (University of Southern California); and the epitome of that dissertation in 'Tolkien's Creative Technique: *Beowulf* and *The Hobbit*', *Orcrist*, 7 (1972–73) 16–20; and William Howard Green's '*The Hobbit* and Other Fiction by J. R. R. Tolkien: Their Roots in Medieval Heroic Literature and Language', *DAI*, 30 (1970) 4944A (Louisiana State University). On medieval ideas in *The Lord of the Rings* see for example John Tinkler, 'Old English in Rohan', *Tolkien and the Critics*, ed. Neil D. Isaacs and Rose A. Zimbardo (Notre Dame and London: University of Notre Dame Press, 1968) pp. 164–9; Sandra L. Miesel, 'Some Motifs and Sources for *Lord of the Rings*', *Riverside Quarterly*, 3 (1968) 125–8; E. L. Epstein, 'The Novels of J. R. R. Tolkien and the Ethnology of Medieval Christendom', *Philological Quarterly*, 48 (1969) 517–25; and Lin Carter, *Tolkien: A Look Behind The Lord of the Rings* (New York: Ballantine, 1969).

7. 'Beowulf: The Monsters and the Critics', *Proceedings of the British Academy*, 22 (1936) 245–95, rpt. in *An Anthology of Beowulf Criticism*, ed. Lewis E. Nicholson (Notre Dame: University of Notre Dame Press, 1963), and in *The Beowulf Poet*, ed. Donald K. Fry (Englewood Cliffs, New Jersey: Prentice-Hall, 1968). All references derive from the Nicholson anthology (here, p. 85).

8. 'On Fairy-Stories', *Essays Presented to Charles Williams*, ed. C. S. Lewis (London; Oxford University Press, 1947, and Grand Rapids, Michigan: William B. Eerdmans, 1966) pp. 38–89; rev. and rpt. in *Tree and Leaf* (London: Allen & Unwin, 1964; Boston: Houghton Mifflin, 1965); rpt. in *The Tolkien Reader*, p. 68–70.

9. For a definition of medieval tragedy and its Chaucerian application see D. W. Robertson, Jr., 'Chaucerian Tragedy', *ELH*, 19 (1952), 1–37; rpt. in *Chaucer Criticism*, Vol. II: *Troilus and Criseyde and the Minor Poems*, ed. Richard J. Schoeck and Jerome Taylor (Notre Dame: University of Notre Dame Press, 1961) pp. 86–121.

10. Kocher, p. 170.

11. Kocher, p. 186. His excellent discussion (pp. 178–95) stresses the work as a scholarly parody rather than as a literary parody of fourteenth-century works or of Tolkien's own creative works, especially *The Hobbit*.

12. See Charles Muscatine, *Chaucer and the French Tradition: A Study in Style and Meaning* (Berkeley and Los Angeles: University of California Press, 1957).

13. Canute has been revealed as especially well-disposed toward the house at Ely, in a study published prior to 'The Homecoming' which Tolkien may have read. Dom David Knowles, in *The Monastic Order in England: A History of its Development from the Times of St Dunstan to the Fourth Lateran Council, 943–1216* (Cambridge: Cambridge University Press, 1949), declares that 'Cnut, once in power, showed himself not only a strong and able ruler, but a patron of the monastic order and the friend of Aethelnoth of Canterbury and other monk-bishops. His reign shows no change in the policy of appointing monks to vacant sees, and Cnut and his chief magnates appear as benefactors to a number of important houses. In

East Anglia, hitherto bare of monasteries, two great foundations owed their origin to the Danish king, St Benet's of Holme, near the coast not far from Norwich, and Bury St Edmunds. Both of these received colonists from Ely, a house for which Cnut always entertained a particular affection . . .' (p. 70).

CHAPTER 5

1. Randel Helms, *Tolkien's World* (Boston: Houghton Mifflin, 1974) p. 21. For the entire analysis of the parallels see Chapter Two, 'Tolkien's Leaf'.

2. For its medieval (and classical) linguistic, literary, and mythological sources, influences, and parallels see, for example, Caroline Whitman Everett, 'The Imaginative Fiction of J. R. R. Tolkien' (M.A., Florida State University, 1957), Chapter Four; Alexis Levitin, 'J. R. R. Tolkien's *The Lord of the Rings*' (M.A., Columbia University, 1964), Chapter Two; John Tinkler, 'Old English in Rohan', in *Tolkien and the Critics*, ed. Neil D. Isaacs and Rose A. Zimbardo (Notre Dame and London: University of Notre Dame Press, 1968) pp. 164–9; Sandra L. Miesel. 'Some Motifs and Sources for *Lord of the Rings*', *Riverside Quarterly*, 3 (1968) 125–8; E. L. Epstein, 'The Novels of J. R. R. Tolkien and the Ethnology of Medieval Christendom', *Philological Quarterly*, 48 (1969) 517–25; Lin Carter, *Tolkien: A Look Behind the Lord of the Rings* (New York: Ballantine, 1969), *passim*; Kenneth J. Reckford, 'Some Trees in Virgil and Tolkien', in *Perspectives of Roman Poetry: A Classics Symposium*, ed. G. Karl Galinsky (Austin and London: University of Texas Press, 1974) pp. 57–92; Charles A. Huttar, 'Hell and the City: Tolkien and the Traditions of Western Literature', in *A Tolkien Compass*, ed. Jared Lobdell (La Salle, Ill.: Open Court Press, 1975) pp. 117–42; and Ruth S. Noel, *The Mythology of Middle-earth* (London: Thames & Hudson, 1977).

3. For religious, moral, or Christian aspects of the trilogy see Edmund Fuller, *Books with Men behind Them* (New York: Random House, 1959, 1961, 1962) pp. 169–96 ('The Lord of the Hobbits: J. R. R. Tolkien'); Patricia Meyer Spacks, 'Ethical Patterns in *The Lord of the Rings*', *Critique*, 3 (1959) 30–42, rpt. as 'Power and Meaning in *The Lord of the Rings*', in *Tolkien and the Critics*, pp. 81–99; Levitin, pp. 87–106 (Chapter Five: 'Inherent Morality and its Concomitants'); Sandra Miesel, 'Some Religious Aspects of *Lord of the Rings*', *Riverside Quarterly*, 3 (1968) 209–13; Gunnar Urang, 'Tolkien's Fantasy: The Phenomenology of Hope', in *Shadows of Imagination: The Fantasies of C. S. Lewis, J. R. R. Tolkien, and Charles Williams*, ed. Mark R. Hillegas (Carbondale and Edwardsville: Southern Illinois University Press, 1969) pp. 97–110; Paul Kocher, *Master of Middle-earth: The Fiction of J. R. R. Tolkien* (Boston: Houghton Mifflin, 1972), Chapter Three: 'Cosmic Order'; and Richard Purtill, *Lord of the Elves and Eldils: Fantasy and Philosophy in C. S. Lewis and J. R. R. Tolkien* (Grand Rapids, Michigan: Zondervan, 1974).

4. Spacks, pp. 83–4.

5. For *The Lord of the Rings* as traditional epic see Bruce A. Beatie, 'Folk Tale, Fiction, and Saga in J. R. R. Tolkien's *The Lord of the Rings*', in 'The Tolkien Papers', *Mankato Studies in English*, 2 (1967) 1–17; as fantasy drawing upon epic, *chanson de geste*, and medieval romance: see Carter, pp. 96–133; as fantasy: see Douglass Parker, 'Hwaet We Holbytla . . .,'

Hudson Review, 9 (1956–57) 598–609; as fairy-story: see R. J. Reilly, 'Tolkien and the Fairy Story', *Thought*, 38 (1963), 89–106, rpt. in *Tolkien and the Critics*, pp. 128–50; as a genreless work: see Charles Moorman, 'The Shire, Mordor, and Minas Tirith', in *Tolkien and the Critics*, pp. 201–2.

6. For Aragorn as hero see Kocher, Chapter Six; for Frodo see Roger Sale, *Modern Heroism: Essays on D. H. Lawrence, William Empson, and J. R. R. Tolkien* (Berkeley, Los Angeles and London: University of California Press, 1973); and for Aragorn as the epic hero and Frodo as the fairy-tale hero see Levitin, pp. 60–76. Because heroism and *ofermod* are incompatible it is difficult to choose 'the Hero' of the work; see Miesel's brief mention of this idea in 'Some Religious Aspects of *Lord of the Rings*', p. 212; further, real heroism depends more on service than mastery, making Sam, who resembles Niggle in 'Leaf by Niggle', the best choice for hero: see Jack C. Rang, 'Two Servants', in 'The Tolkien Papers', pp. 84–94.

7. For other views of structure in the trilogy see, for example, Helms, Chapter Five ('Tolkien's World: The Structure and Aesthetic of *The Lord of the Rings*'); Richard C. West, 'The Interlace Structure of *The Lord of the Rings*', in *A Tolkien Compass*, pp. 77–94; and David M. Miller, 'Narrative Pattern in *The Fellowship of the Ring*', in *A Tolkien Compass*, pp. 95–106.

8. Quoted from a letter appended to Everett's M.A. thesis, p. 87.

9. *The Lord of the Rings*, 3 vols (London: Allen & Unwin, 1954, 1955; Boston: Houghton Mifflin, 1955, 1956, 2nd ed. 1967; rev. ed. New York: Ballantine, 1965; rpt. 1966) I, 231.

10. Boethius, *The Consolation of Philosophy*, trans. Richard Green (Indianapolis, New York, and Kansas City: Bobbs-Merrill, 1962) p. 97 (Book IV, Poem 6).

11. For a classification and discussion of the good species and/or the evil species see Rose A. Zimbardo, 'Moral Vision in *The Lord of the Rings*', in *Tolkien and the Critics*, pp. 100–8; Thomas J. Gasque, 'Tolkien: The Monsters and the Critters', in *Tolkien and the Critics*, pp. 151–63; Robley Evans, *J. R. R. Tolkien* (New York: Warner Paperback Library, 1972), Chapters Three to Five; and Kocher, Chapters Four to Five.

12. For a discussion of the descent into Hell in the second book and its traditional implications see Huttar, pp. 117–42.

13. Alexander Jones (ed.) *The Jerusalem Bible* (Garden City, New York: Doubleday, 1966) p. 26 (11:1–4). Tolkien participated as a principal collaborator (one of twenty-seven) in the translation and literary revision of this Bible.

14. See Tinkler, 'Old English in Rohan', in *Tolkien and the Critics*, pp. 164–9.

15. My translation of lines 92–3. See the original in *The Exeter Book*, Vol. 3 of *The Anglo-Saxon Poetic Records*, ed. George Philip Krapp and Elliott Van Kirk Dobbie (Morningside Heights, New York: Columbia University Press, 1936).

16. For a related discussion of the implications of return and renewal in the last book see Evans, pp. 190–3.

17. See also Rang, 'Two Servants', pp. 84–94.

CONCLUSION
1. Humphrey Carpenter, *J. R. R. Tolkien: A Biography* (London, Boston, and Sydney: Allen & Unwin, 1977) p. 89.
2. Carpenter, pp. 251–2.
3. Carpenter, p. 107.
4. Carpenter, p. 184.
5. Carpenter, p. 210.
6. Carpenter, p. 251.
7. J. R. R. Tolkien, *The Silmarillion*, ed. Christopher Tolkien (London: Allen & Unwin; Boston: Houghton Mifflin, 1977) p. 54. Subsequent references will be indicated within the text.

Select Bibliography

PRINCIPAL WORKS OF J. R. R. TOLKIEN

A Middle English Vocabulary (Oxford: Clarendon Press, 1922).

'Some Contributions to Middle-English Lexicography', *Review of English Studies*, 1 (1925) 210–15.

'The Devil's Coach-Horses', *Review of English Studies*, 1 (1925) 331–6.

Sir Gawain and the Green Knight, co-ed. E. V. Gordon, 2nd ed. rev. Norman Davis (1925, 1960; rpt. Oxford: Clarendon Press, 1967).

Foreword to *A New Glossary of the Dialect of the Huddersfield District*, by Walter E. Haigh (London: Oxford University Press, 1928).

'*Ancrene Wisse* and *Hali Meiðhad*', *Essays and Studies by Members of the English Association*, 14 (1929) 104–26.

'Sigelwara Land', Part 1 in *Medium Aevum*, 1 (1932) 183–96; ·Part 2 in *Medium Aevum*, 3 (1934) 95–111.

'Chaucer as Philologist: The Reeve's Tale', *Transactions of the Philological Society* (1934) pp. 1–70.

'Beowulf: The Monsters and the Critics', *Proceedings of the British Academy*, 22 (1936) 245–95. Rpt. in *An Anthology of Beowulf Criticism*, ed. Lewis E. Nicholson (Notre Dame, Indiana: University of Notre Dame Press, 1963); and in *The Beowulf Poet*, ed. Donald K. Fry. (Englewood Cliffs, New Jersey: Prentice-Hall, 1968).

The Hobbit; or There and Back Again (London: Allen & Unwin, 1937, 1951; Boston: Houghton Mifflin, 1938, 1958; New York: Ballantine, 1965, rpt. 1974).

Letter to the Editor, *The Observer* (20 February 1938) p. 9.

Preface to *Beowulf and the Finnesburg Fragment: A Translation into Modern English Prose*, by John R. Clark Hall (London: Allen & Unwin, 1940).

'Leaf by Niggle', *Dublin Review*, 216 (1945) 46–61; rpt. in *Tree and Leaf* (London: Allen & Unwin, 1964; Boston: Houghton Mifflin, 1965); and in *The Tolkien Reader* (New York: Ballantine, 1966; rpt. 1975).

'The Lay of Aotrou and Itroun', *Welsh Review*, 4 (1945) 254–66.

'On Fairy-Stories.' *Essays Presented to Charles Williams*, ed. C. S. Lewis (London: Oxford University Press, 1947) pp. 38–89; (Grand Rapids, Michigan: William B. Eerdmans, 1966) pp. 38–89; rev. and rpt. in *Tree and Leaf* (London: Allen & Unwin, 1964; Boston: Houghton Mifflin, 1965); and in *The Tolkien Reader* (New York: Ballantine, 1966; rpt. 1975).

Farmer Giles of Ham (London: Allen & Unwin, 1949; Boston: Houghton Mifflin, 1950). Rpt. in *The Tolkien Reader* (New York: Ballantine, 1966; rpt. 1975); and *Smith of Wootton Major and Farmer Giles of Ham* (New York: Ballantine, 1969; rpt. 1975).

'Middle English "Losenger": Sketch of an Etymological and Semantic Enquiry', *Essais de Philologie Moderne* (Paris: Société d'édition 'Les Belles Lettres', 1953).

'The Homecoming of Beorhtnoth Beorhthelm's Son', *Essays and Studies by Members of the English Association*, N.S. 6 (1953) 1–18; rpt. in *The Tolkien Reader* (New York: Ballantine, 1966; rpt. 1975).

The Lord of the Rings (3 vols) (London: Allen & Unwin, 1954, 1955; Boston: Houghton Mifflin, 1955, 1956, 2nd ed. 1967; rev. ed. New York: Ballantine, 1965; rpt. 1966).

'Imram', *Time and Tide*, 36 (1955) 1561.

Preface to *The Ancrene Riwle*, trans. M. B. Salu (London: Burns & Oates, 1955; Notre Dame: University of Notre Dame Press, 1956).

The English Text of the Ancrene Riwle: Ancrene Wisse, Early English Text Society, No. 249 (London, New York, and Toronto: Oxford University Press, 1962).

The Adventures of Tom Bombadil (London: Allen & Unwin, 1962; Boston: Houghton Mifflin, 1962; rpt. in *The Tolkien Reader*. New York: Ballantine, 1966; rpt. 1975).

'English and Welsh', in *Angles and Britons: The O'Donnell Lectures* (Cardiff: University of Wales Press, 1963).

The Tolkien Reader (New York: Ballantine, 1966; rpt. 1975).

The Road Goes Ever On: A Song Cycle (London: Allen & Unwin, 1967; Boston: Houghton Mifflin, 1967).

Smith of Wootton Major (London: Allen & Unwin, 1967; Boston: Houghton Mifflin, 1967); *Redbook*, 130 (1967) 58–61, 101, 103–7; rpt. in *Smith of Wootton Major and Farmer Giles of Ham* (New York: Ballantine, 1969; rpt. 1975).

'For W. H. A.', *Shenandoah*, 18 (1967) 96–7.

Smith of Wootton Major and Farmer Giles of Ham (New York: Ballantine, 1969; rpt. 1975).

'A Letter from J. R. R. Tolkien', in William Luther White, *The Image of Man in C. S. Lewis* (Nashville: Abingdon Press, 1969).

'Upon a Time', and 'The Dragon's Visit', in *The Young Magicians*, ed. Lin Carter (New York: Ballantine, 1969).

Trans. *Sir Gawain and the Green Knight, Pearl, and Sir Orfeo*, ed. Christopher Tolkien (London: Allen & Unwin, 1975; Boston: Houghton Mifflin, 1975).

The Father Christmas Letters, ed. Baillie Tolkien (London: Allen & Unwin, 1976; Boston: Houghton Mifflin, 1976).

The Silmarillion, ed. Christopher Tolkien (London: Allen & Unwin; Boston: Houghton Mifflin, 1977).

OTHER PRIMARY AND SECONDARY WORKS

St Augustine, *On Christian Doctrine*, trans. D. W. Robertson, Jr (Indianapolis and New York: Bobbs-Merrill, 1958).

Avery, Gillian, *Nineteenth-Century Children: Heroes and Heroines in English Children's Stories 1780–1900* (London: Hodder & Stoughton, 1965).

Blissett, William, 'The Despots of the Rings', *The South Atlantic Quarterly*, 58 (1959) 448–56.

Bloomfield, Morton W., *The Seven Deadly Sins: An Introduction to the History of a Religious Concept* (East Lansing: Michigan State College Press, 1952).

Boas, George, *Essays on Primitivism and Related Ideas in the Middle Ages* (Baltimore: Johns Hopkins University Press, 1948).

Boethius, *The Consolation of Philosophy*, trans. Richard Green (Indianapolis, New York, and Kansas City: Bobbs-Merrill, 1962).

Carpenter, Humphrey, *J. R. R. Tolkien: A Biography* (London, Boston, and Sydney: Allen & Unwin, 1977).

Carter, Lin, *Tolkien: A Look Behind The Lord of the Rings* (New York: Ballantine, 1969).

Chaucer, Geoffrey, *Works*, ed. F. N. Robinson, 2nd ed (Boston: Houghton Mifflin, 1957).

Christensen, Bonniejean, '*Beowulf* and *The Hobbit*: Elegy into Fantasy in J. R. R. Tolkien's Creative Technique', *DAI*, 30 (1970) 4401A–4402A (University of Southern California).

——, 'Tolkien's Creative Technique: *Beowulf* and *The Hobbit*', *Orcrist*, 7 (1972–73) 16–20.

Conley, John (ed.), *The Middle English Pearl: Critical Essays* (Notre Dame and London: University of Notre Dame Press, 1970).

Cursor Mundi, ed. Rev. Richard Morris. Early English Text Society, O.S. No. 57, 59, 62, 66, 68, 99, 101 (London: Kegan Paul, Trench, Trübner, 1874–93).

Epstein, E. L. 'The Novels of J. R. R. Tolkien and the Ethnology of Medieval Christendom', *Philological Quarterly*, 48 (1969) 517–25.

Evans, Robley, *J. R. R. Tolkien* (New York: Warner Paperback Library, 1972).

Everett, Caroline Whitman, 'The Imaginative Fiction of J. R. R. Tolkien' (M.A. Florida State University, 1957).

The Exeter Book, The Anglo-Saxon Poetic Records, vol. 3, ed. George Philip Krapp and Elliott Van Kirk Dobbie (Morningside Heights, New York: Columbia University Press, 1936).

Foster, Robert, *A Guide to Middle-Earth* (New York: Ballantine, 1971).

Fuller, Edmund, *Books with Men behind Them* (New York: Random House, 1959, 1961, 1962).

Gilson, Étienne, *Reason and Revelation in the Middle Ages* (1938; rpt. New York: Charles Scribner's Sons, 1966).

Green, Roger Lancelyn, and Walter Hooper, *C. S. Lewis: A Biography* (New York and London: Harcourt Brace Jovanovich, 1974).

Green, William Howard, '*The Hobbit* and Other Fiction by J. R. R. Tolkien: Their Roots in Medieval Heroic Literature and Language', *DAI*, 30 (1970) 4944A (Louisiana State University).

Grotta-Kurska, Daniel, *J. R. R. Tolkien: Architect of Middle Earth*, ed. Frank Wilson (Philadelphia: Running Press, 1976).

Helms, Randel, *Tolkien's World* (Boston: Houghton Mifflin, 1974).

Hillegas, Mark R. (ed.), *Shadows of the Imagination: The Fantasies of C. S. Lewis, J. R. R. Tolkien, and Charles Williams* (Carbondale and Edwardsville: Southern Illinois University Press, 1969).

Huttar, Charles A., *Imagination and the Spirit: Essays in Literature and the Christian Faith presented to Clyde S. Kilby* (Grand Rapids, Mich.: William B. Eerdmans, 1971).

Irwin, W. R., 'There and Back Again: The Romances of Williams, Lewis and Tolkien', *Sewanee Review*, 69 (1961) 566–78.

Isaacs, Neil D., and Rose A. Zimbardo (ed.), *Tolkien and the Critics: Essays on J. R. R. Tolkien's The Lord of the Rings* (Notre Dame and London: University of Notre Dame Press, 1968).

Johnson, J. A., '*Farmer Giles of Ham*: What is It?' *Orcrist*, 7 (1972–73) 21–4.

Jones, Alexander (ed.), *The Jerusalem Bible* (Garden City, New York: Doubleday, 1966).

Knowles, Dom David, *The Monastic Order in England: A History of its Development from the Times of St Dunstan to the Fourth Lateran Council, 943-1216* (Cambridge: Cambridge University Press, 1949).

Kocher, Paul H., *Master of Middle-earth: The Fiction of J. R. R. Tolkien* (Boston: Houghton Mifflin, 1972).

Levitin, Alexis, 'J. R. R. Tolkien's *The Lord of the Rings*' (M. A., Columbia University, 1964).

Lewis, C. S., *Letters*, ed. W. H. Lewis (1966; rpt. New York and London: Harcourt Brace Jovanovich, 1975).

Lewis, Lionel S., *Scaling the Ivory Tower: Merit and its Limits in Academic Careers* (Baltimore and London: Johns Hopkins University Press, 1975).

Lobdell, Jared (ed.), *A Tolkien Compass* (La Salle, Ill.: Open Court Press, 1975).

Macrobius, *Commentary on the Dream of Scipio*, trans. William Harris Stahl (1952; rpt. New York and London: Columbia University Press, 1966).

Miesel, Sandra L., 'Some Motifs and Sources for *Lord of the Rings*', *Riverside Quarterly*, 3 (1968) 125–8.

——, 'Some Religious Aspects of *Lord of the Rings*', *Riverside Quarterly*, 3 (1968) 209–13.

Muscatine, Charles, *Chaucer and the French Tradition: A Study in Style and Meaning* (Berkeley and Los Angeles: University of California Press, 1957).

Nitzsche, Jane Chance, *The Genius Figure in Antiquity and the Middle Ages* (New York and London: Columbia University Press, 1975).

——, 'Mythology for England: Tolkien's *Silmarillion*', *Houston Chronicle*, Sunday *Zest Section* (11 Sept 1977), p. 13.

Noel, Ruth S., *The Mythology of Middle-earth: A Study of Tolkien's Mythology and its Relationship to the Myths of the Ancient World* (London: Thames & Hudson, 1977).

Norman, Philip, 'The Prevalence of Hobbits', *The New York Times Magazine* (15 Jan 1967) pp. 30–1, 97, 100, 102.

Parker, Douglass, 'Hwaet We Holbytla . . .' (review of *Lord of the Rings*), *Hudson Review*, 9 (1956–57) 598–609.

Purtill, Richard, *Lord of the Elves and Eldils: Fantasy and Philosophy in C. S. Lewis and J. R. R. Tolkien* (Grand Rapids, Mich.: Zondervan, 1974).

Ready, William, *Understanding Tolkien and The Lord of the Rings* (New York: Warner Paperback Library, 1969).

Reckford, Kenneth J., 'Some Trees in Virgil and Tolkien.' In *Perspectives of Roman Poetry: A Classics Symposium*, ed. G. Karl Galinsky (Austin and London: University of Texas Press, 1974).

Robertson, D. W., Jr., 'Chaucerian Tragedy', *ELH*, 19 (1952), 1–37; rpt. in *Chaucer Criticism*, vol. II: *Troilus and Criseyde and the Minor Poems*, ed. Richard J. Schoeck and Jerome Taylor (Notre Dame: University of Notre Dame Press, 1961).

St Clair, Gloria Ann Strange Slaughter, 'Studies in the Sources of J. R. R. Tolkien's *The Lord of the Rings*', *DAI*, 30 (1970) 5001A (Oklahoma).

Sale, Roger, *Modern Heroism: Essays on D. H. Lawrence, William Empson and J. R. R. Tolkien* (Berkeley, Los Angeles, and London: University of California Press, 1973).

Stimpson, Catharine R., *J. R. R. Tolkien*, Columbia Essays on Modern Writers, no. 41 (New York and London: Columbia University Press, 1969).

Thomson, George H., '*The Lord of the Rings*: The Novel as Traditional Romance', *Wisconsin Studies in Contemporary Literature*, 8 (1967) 43–59.

West, Richard C., *Tolkien Criticism: An Annotated Checklist* (Kent, Ohio: Kent State University Press, 1970).

Wetherbee, Winthrop *Platonism and Poetry in the Twelfth Century: The Literary Influence of the School of Chartres* (Princeton: Princeton University Press, 1972).

Wilson, Colin, *Tree by Tolkien* (London: Covent Garden Press, 1973; Santa Barbara, Calif.: Capra Press, 1974).

Wilson, Edmund, 'Oo, Those Awful Orcs!' *Nation*, 182 (1956) 312–13, rpt. in *The Bit between My Teeth: A Literary Chronicle of 1950—1965* (New York: Farrar, Straus & Giroux, 1965).

Index

(God, cont.)

Genesis, 112; disobedience to, in *The Two Towers*, 115; Eru like, in *The Silmarillion*, 133

Goldberry, 107–8

Gollum (Smeagol): in *The Hobbit*, 6, 31–48 *passim*, 86, 138*n*2, 139*n*5; in *The Lord of the Rings*, 6–7, 22, 29, 101–2, 105–6, 116–18

Gondor, 112, 119–20, 121, 124, 126, 132

Good Works, 59

Gordon, E. V., 16

Gospels, 52–5, 67

Great Cake, 68, 72

Green Knight, 87

Green, William Howard, 139*n*5

Grendel: as monster, 4, 8–10, 51; as adversary of the critic, 12; the critic like, 13, 23–4; like Satan, 24; Beowulf like, 32; Gollum like, 35, 139*n*5; Bilbo like, 40; the giant in *Farmer Giles of Ham* like, 86

Grendel's Mother, 139*n*5

Grey Company, 120

Grey Havens, 124

Grisnákh, 113–14

Grubb, Grubb, and Burrowes, 39, 67

Gulliver, 20

Gulliver's Travels, 20

Guyon, Sir, 52

halflings, *see* hobbits

Hali Meiðhad, 2, 18

Ham (place), 86

Hama, 117

Heaven: secondary world of fantasy like, 24, 29; Faërie like, 28, 50, 53; in 'Leaf by Niggle', 61; in 'The Lay of Aotrou and Itroun', 84; in 'Imram', 95

Hell, 26, 50, 58, 95, 113

Helms, Randel, 1, 97–8, 135*n*1, 138*n*1

Helm's Deep, 118

Heorot, 24, 40, 86

Historia, 10

'Historia Eliensis', 92

Hobbit, The: and *The Silmarillion*, 2, 129, 130, 131, 134; sources of, 2, 3, 5, 139*n*6; and *Beowulf*, 2, 56, 80, 86, 135–6*n*1, 138–9*n*5; title of, 4; narrator of, 5, 31–48 *passim*, 69, 86; and 'Beowulf: The Monsters and the Critics', 5, 11, 56, 86, 100, 31–48 *passim*; and 'On Fairy-Stories', 5, 31–48 *passim*; monsters in, 5, 31–48 *passim*; writing of, 20; divided self in, 29, 31–48 *passim*; and *Ancrene Wisse*, 31–48 *passim*, 57, 100; and 'Smith of Wootton Major', 54, 69, 70; and 'Leaf by Niggle', 57, 60; and the medieval parodies, 75–6, 77; and *Farmer Giles of Ham*, 85, 86; and 'The Homecoming of Beorhtnoth', 93, 94; and *The Lord of the Rings*, 97–8, 126, 138*n*2, 138*n*3; and *The Fellowship of the Ring*, 99, 101; and *The Two Towers*, 99, 100; and *The Return of the King*, 119; subtitle of, and Tolkien's works, 127

Hobbiton, 34

hobbits, 1, 11, 18–19, 31–48 *passim*, 97–127 *passim*

'Homecoming of Beorhtnoth Beorhthelm's Son, The': title of, 4; Germanic lord in, 4, 6, 75–81 *passim*, 90–4; divided self in, 29, 90–4; as medieval parody, 75–81 *passim*, 90–4; and *Farmer Giles of Ham*, 85–7; and *Sir Gawain and the Green Knight*, 87; and *The Lord of the Rings*, 126

House Inspector, 61

House of the Dead, 123

House of Healing, 4, 123

Hrothgar, 10, 24, 97

Hygd, 34

Hyginus, 130

Ilúvatar, *see* Eru

imram, 75, 94–5

'Imram', 6, 75–7, 94–6

Incarnation, 29, 52, 71, 115

incubus, 70

164

INDEX

(Tolkien, J. R. R., *cont*.)

7, 9–23, 29–30, 55, 135–6n1; as editor of *Ancrene Wisse*, in his Prefatory Note, 16; as editor of *Sir Gawain and the Green Knight*, in his Preface, 16; as translator of the *Pearl* poet, in his Preface, 17, 18, 136n8; as *Beowulf*-scholar, in his Prefatory Remarks to the Clark Hall translation, 17; as philologist, in '*Ancrene Wisse* and *Hali Meiðhad*', 18; as philologist, in the Appendices and Prologue to *The Lord of the Rings*, 20–3; as philologist, in his Preface to Salu's translation of *Ancrene Wisse*, 33; as literary theorist, and early life of, 50; as fairy-story writer, and autobiography of, 56, 140n6; as artist and critic, unified ideas of, 126–7; as philologist, in *The Silmarillion*, 129–30; as translator of Jerusalem Bible, 144n13

Tompkins, 11, 56, 62, 64, 65

Took, Adelard, 105

Tooks, 29, 41–2, 45, 47, 94, 103

Torhthelm, 29, 90–4

Tower of Babel, 12, 112

tragedy, 35, 51, 76–7, 141n1, 142n9

Tree and Leaf, 16, 25–6, 55–6, 137n15. See also 'Leaf by Niggle'; 'On Fairy-Stories'

Treebeard, 114

Tree of Knowledge of Good and Evil, 25, 26, 58, 106

Tree of Life, 26, 50, 52, 58, 73

Tree of Tales, 25

Trinity, 65

tristia, 33

Troilus and Criseyde, 77

trolls, 33, 37–8, 41, 43, 47

Twelfth Night, 89

Two Towers, The, 99, 100, 111–18, 137n16. See also *The Lord of the Rings*

Two Trees, 131, 132

tyrannus, see rex iniustus

ubi sunt, 117

Uglúk, 114

Underhill, 34, 39

underworld, 50, 58–9, 106–8, 141n16. See also Hell

Unferth, 139n5

Ungoliant, 133

United Kingdom, 77. See also Britain; Little Kingdom

Unwin, Raynor, 129

Unwin, Stanley, 129

Uruk-hai, 113–14

Vala(r), 103, 129–32

ventris ingluvies, 33

vetus homo, 26–7, 29, 70, 94, 104, 119

Vita Nuova, La, 84

Voice in the Dark, 80, 93, 94. See also Canute, King

'Voyage of Earendel the Evening Star, The', 2

'Voyage of St Brendan, The', see *Navigatio Sancti Brendani Abbatis*

'Wanderer, The', 117

Wanley, Humphrey, 10

wargs, 33, 37, 38, 41

Welsh, 2

Westron, 109

White, G. H., 135n7, 139n6

Wiglaf, 32, 79, 86

Wild Men, 120

Wood-elves, 38–9, 41, 48

Wootton Major, 68–9, 71

Word of God, 6, 24, 25–9, 53, 71, 92. See also Bible; Christ

Wordsworth, William, 14

Workhouse, 58–9, 62, 63, 64, 66

World Soul, 59

World War, First, 21

World War, Second, 21

Worm, 25, 125. See also Wormtongue

Wormtongue, 25, 113–15, 122

Yavanna, 131